Anatole Claudin

The First Paris Press

An Account of the Books Printed for G. Fichet and J. Heynlin in the

Sorbonne, 1470-1472

Anatole Claudin

The First Paris Press
An Account of the Books Printed for G. Fichet and J. Heynlin in the Sorbonne, 1470-1472

ISBN/EAN: 9783337250973

Printed in Europe, USA, Canada, Australia, Japan

Cover: Foto ©ninafisch / pixelio.de

More available books at **www.hansebooks.com**

Sanctissimo patri Sixto Quarto pontifici maximo, Guillermus fichetus, universitatis theologorum Parisiensium doctorum, devota pedum oscula.

THE FIRST PARIS PRESS

AN ACCOUNT OF THE BOOKS PRINTED
FOR G. FICHET AND J. HEYNLIN
IN THE SORBONNE
1470—1472

BY A. CLAUDIN

LONDON
PRINTED FOR THE BIBLIOGRAPHICAL SOCIETY
AT THE CHISWICK PRESS
FEBRUARY 1898 FOR 1897

CONTENTS.

	PAGE

FRONTISPIECE: Miniature showing Fichet presenting a copy of his *Rhetoric* to Pope Sixtus IV., from the presentation copy to the Pope now in the British Museum.

TEXT 1

NOTES . 35

BIBLIOGRAPHY 49
    I. Gasparini Epistolæ 49
    II. Gasparini Orthographia . . . 50
    III. Sallustius 51
    IV. Florus 52
    V. Bessarionis Orationes . . . 52
    VI. Ficheti Rhetorica 53
    VII. Augustini Dati Eloquentiæ Præcepta . . 56
  [VIII. Cicero De Oratore] . . . 56
  [IX. Valerius Maximus] . . . 56
    X. Vallæ Elegantiæ 57
    XI. Cicero. De Officiis, etc. . . 58
    XII. Cicero. Tusculanæ Quæstiones . 60
    XIII. Rodericus Zamorensis, Speculum Humanæ Vitæ 61
    XIV. Platonis Epistolæ . . . 62
    XV. Phalaridis, Bruti et Crati Epistolæ . . 63
    XVI. Virgilius Maro. Bucolica, etc. . . 64
  XVII. Juvenalis et Persii Satyræ . . 65
XVIII. Terentius 65
    XIX. Aeneas Sylvius. De duobus Amantibus . 66
    XX. Aeneas Sylvius. De Curialium Miseria . 66
    XXI. Sophologium Jacobi Magni . . . 67
    XXII. Ambrosius, De Officiis; Seneca, De Quatuor Virtutibus . . 68

	PAGE
DOCUMENTS	71
I. Letter of Fichet to Jean de la Pierre (Johann Heynlin), from the *Epistolæ Gasparini*	71
II. Letter of Fichet to Gaguin, from the *Orthographia*	72
III. Letter of presentation to Cardinal Rolin, from the *Orationes Bessarionis*	75
IV. Letter of presentation to Cardinal Rolin, from Fichet's *Rhetorica*	76
V. Letter of presentation to Guillaume Chartier, Bishop of Paris, also from the *Rhetorica*	76
VI. Letter of Senilis to Heynlin, from the *Valla*	77
VII. Letter of acknowledgment from Heynlin to Senilis	78
VIII. Letter of presentation from Heynlin to George, Bishop of Metz, from the *Cicero de Officiis*	79
IX. Letter of Fichet to Heynlin, from the same	80
X. Letter of Heynlin to Fichet, from the same	82
XI. Letter of presentation to Robert D'Estouteville, from the *Rodericus Zamorensis*	83
XII. Letter of presentation to the Duc de Bourbon, from the same	84
XIII. Letter of presentation to the King, from the same	85
XIV. Letter of Fichet to Jean Choard, from the *Epistolæ Platonis*	87
FACSIMILES	91
First page of the *Epistolæ Gasparini*	91
Last page, with colophon, from the same	92
First four pages of the letter from Fichet to Gaguin, from the *Orthographia*	93
First page of the *Sallust*	97
Last page, with colophon, from the same	98
Letter to the Duc de Bourbon, from the *Rodericus Zamorensis*	99
Alphabet of the Sorbonne types	100

*** The four pages from the *Orthographia* are reproduced with the help of plates kindly lent by the Société de l'Histoire de Paris.

THE FIRST PARIS PRESS.

HE history of the first Paris press has **exercised** the skill of many bibliographers during the last two hundred years. The first who dealt systematically with the subject was André Chevillier, librarian of the College of the Sorbonne. He had at his disposal the copies, preserved in the house as relics, of the first impressions executed there : he also had access to the archives of the Congregation. It was not then possible to compare other copies of the same books scattered in numerous libraries and to note their variations ; and he took it for granted that the Sorbonne possessed copies of all the books issued from its early press. For more than a century after the publication of his work, Chevillier was followed by everyone. The Rev. William Parr Greswell[1] made a concise and judicious compilation from him and Panzer, drawing the attention of English readers to early French typography, " a subject of particular curiosity," as he styles it. Since then, other books from the same press have been discovered. Dibdin, Brunet, and Auguste Bernard noticed some of them, Madden and Philippe increased the list.

Starting from these results we have studied the matter afresh. We have compared the copies, and read attentively all the prefaces, which give particulars hitherto unknown or imperfectly understood; and pursuing our inquiry we have examined manuscript documents which had not received serious attention. From these sources of information, combined with known historical facts, we have been able to correct certain erroneous statements generally accepted as trustworthy, and to clear up some obscurities. We give a new classification, which we believe to be final, for all those undated books which have so long baffled the sagacity of bibliographers, and we present the problem in another aspect, chiefly by the help of documents as yet unpublished or wrongly interpreted. With these introductory remarks, we proceed at once to the investigation of our subject.

In our opinion, the first press erected in the precincts of the old Sorbonne was not a public printing establishment set up as a speculation, but was in reality a private press worked by professional printers, specially brought to Paris for the purpose, under the direction of its owner and promoter. Neither the Society of the Sorbonne as a body, nor the king, had anything to do with the introduction of printing, as is generally believed.

The prior elected for the year 1470, Johann Heynlin, alias de la Pierre (de Lapide),[2] who had the year before been rector of the University,[3] was a great lover of books. Desiring to impart to scholars the benefits of the new invention and to multiply good texts, he communicated his ideas on the subject to one of the most eminent of the professors, his friend Guillaume Fichet, "a person of great enterprise, reading, and eloquence,"[33] who had also been rector, and who was at the time librarian of the Sorbonne. Fichet, with the aid of a wealthy and generous protector, agreed to support the first expenses of the establishment thus contemplated. In consequence of this arrangement, Heynlin invited from Basel, where he had gone through the university course and had seen the typographical art exercised, three persons who, he intended, should establish the first printing-press in France. His invitation was readily accepted. The names of the three partners in order were: Michael Freyburger, of Colmar in Elsass, the head of the firm, Master in the Faculty of Arts[4] of the University of Basel, an old acquaintance of Heynlin, and two craftsmen, very likely younger men, Ulrich Gering, of Constanz in Baden,[5] and Martin Crantz.[6]

Sufficient space was contrived for their tools and materials in one of the rooms of the old building[7] reserved for the library, at the back of the adjoining houses of the "grant rue S. Jacques;" the men themselves lodged in the neighbourhood.

They set to work immediately to engrave puncheons and strike matrices, producing a fount of a large, round character, suited to the failing eyesight of the prior.[8] This type was chosen from printed books in Heynlin's possession, being closely imitated from the edition of Caesar's Commentaries, printed at Rome in 1469 by Sweynheim and Pannartz.[9]

The first book issued from the new press was the collection of letters written by Gasparino Barzizi of Bergamo, exhibiting the purest examples of Latin style and elegant diction. The text was carefully revised by Heynlin himself, and was very correctly printed.

Fichet, who rendered Heynlin such effective assistance in the realization of his literary scheme, was a man of great capacity and highly thought of. At the beginning of the year 1469, and again in January, 1470, he had been sent by the king on a secret diplomatic mission[10] to Italy. Guillaume Chartier, Bishop of Paris, had procured him the ecclesiastical benefice of Aunay (Alnetum).[11] The Cardinal Jehan Rolin, Bishop of Autun, a man of literary tastes, held him in high esteem. He had been his protector since he was a youth, and for many years[12] had supplied him liberally with money. Fichet was accordingly in a position—much more so than Heynlin—to contribute materially to the initial outlay. And so, without assistance from the fellows (socii) of the Sorbonne, a society of " poor masters,"[13] who were often in need of money and who could not possibly entertain strangers, Heynlin and Fichet took upon themselves, one the active direction and the other the financial burden of the enterprise.[14]

Their confidence and their enthusiasm for the marvellous art which they had introduced into their adopted city [15] is fully expressed in the metrical colophon to the edition of Gasparino's Letters, in which they ask the patronage of the royal city of Paris, mother of the Muses, for their almost divine art:

> Ut sol lumen, sic doctrinam fundis in orbem,
> Musarum nutrix, regia Parisius.
> Hinc prope divinam tu quam Germania novit
> Artem scribendi suscipe promerita.
> Primos ecce libros quos hæc industria finxit
> Francorum in terris, ædibus atque tuis
> Michael, Udalricus, Martinusque magistri
> Hos impresserunt et facient alios.

There is no date to the volume [16] (a small quarto of 118 leaves, twenty-two lines to the page); but we can easily ascertain it by the preface. This preface consists of a letter addressed by Fichet to his collaborator "Joanni Lapidano Sorbonensis scholae priori." Heynlin is here entitled "prior," and it is said that he had already presided with great credit at the theological discussions of the Sorbonne.[17] The direction of these discussions was one of the special duties of the prior. We may infer then that two or three months at least had passed since his election at the end of March, 1470; and that the printing was finished in the summer, about July or August of that year.[18]

In his letter Fichet thanks Heynlin for the charming Letters of Gasparino which he had sent him in proof. "They are not only carefully corrected by yourself, but also neatly and daintily reproduced by the German printers whom we owe to you.[19] . . . The stationers whom you have brought from your native Germany to Paris turn out copies most exactly corrected after their originals.[20] . . . You strain every nerve to ensure their printing nothing that you have not previously collated in many copies and corrected extensively."[21]

The second book they printed was another work of the same Gasparino, a treatise on the orthography of Latin words arranged alphabetically, entitled, *Gasparini Pergamensis orthographiae liber*. Heynlin added to it nine printed leaves, containing a little tract on diphthongs (de diphthongis) by Guarini of Verona, and a dialogue of his own composition on the art of punctuation (de arte punctandi).[22] Some early copies were issued without these additions.[23] The last sheet was still in the press when Fichet sent a copy, accompanied by a congratulatory letter, as a New Year's gift to Robert Gaguin, a former pupil of his, who had already distinguished himself.

This letter, highly interesting for the particulars it contains, was unknown to bibliographers until it was discovered by myself, printed in the copy which belonged to Heynlin. It is now preserved, along with many others of Heynlin's books, in the University Library at Basel. No other copy containing this letter has as yet been found.

After speaking of the prostrate and decayed state of Latin poetry and eloquence when he arrived years before from his native country to study the philosophy of Aristotle at the School of Paris, Fichet extols the great improvement since made in studies of all sorts. It is partly due to the printers. These studies, he writes, "have derived much light from the new kind of book-producers, whom in our own time Germany, like another Trojan horse, has discharged upon the world (quibus, quantum ipse conjectura capio, magnum lumen novorum librariorum genus attulit, quos nostra memoria sicut quidam equus Trojanus quoquo versus effudit Germania). They tell us that there (in Germany), not far from the city of Mainz (Ferunt enim illic, haut procul a civitate Moguntia), the art of printing was first of all invented by one John, whose surname was Gutenberg (Joannem quemdam fuisse cui cognomen Bonemontano qui primus omnium impressoriam artem excogitaverit)."

Here then is the first authentic statement of the claim of Gutenberg[24] to be the real inventor of printing, a statement indisputably of the highest value as evidence in the case. We pass over the laudatory expressions bestowed by Fichet on the discoverer of so divine an art, to quote what he says concerning the printers of the Sorbonne. "And here particularly I will not omit to mention our own workmen, who now in skill surpass their master: of whom Ulric, Michael, and Martin are said to be the chief (Neque praesertim hoc loco nostros silebo qui superant jam arte magistrum, quorum Udalricus, Michael,[25] ac Martinus principes esse dicuntur). They have already printed the letters of Gasparino of Bergamo, corrected by Jean de la Pierre (qui jam pridem Gasparini Pergamensis epistolas impresserunt quas Joannes Lapidanus emendavit); and now they are exerting themselves to finish the same author's Orthography, also carefully corrected by the same hand (Quin illius auctoris Orthographiam, quam hic etiam accurate correxit, se accingunt perficere)." The letter is subscribed: "At the house of the Sorbonne, written hastily on New Year's Day at daybreak (Aedibus Sorbone raptim a me Kalendis Januariis diluculo scriptum)."

Fichet's present, received by Gaguin on the last day of December, is acknowledged by him in a Latin poem of twenty-four verses (twelve distichs) in praise of Fichet, dated from the convent of the Mathurins, the first of January. This poem is printed after Fichet's letter.

The book itself is a thick volume, nearly double the size of its predecessor, consisting of 221 leaves, including two blank leaves at the beginning and one at the end, for the Orthography; ten leaves, including a final blank leaf, for the two other little treatises; and six leaves, including a final blank, for the letter and Gaguin's verses; or 237 leaves for the complete book. It is printed with twenty-three, instead of twenty-two lines to the page. The type, the same as that employed for the Letters of Gasparino, seems quite new.

From a careful examination of the volume, we are strongly of opinion that the *Orthographia* is in chronological order the second work that issued from the press of the Sorbonne, and that the whole book was completed and the printing finished early in January, 1471.

We are aware that Philippe assigns the completion of the volume to the beginning of 1472; but he has entirely neglected to examine the type, and is consequently unaware of the technical evidence derived from its fresh condition. He confesses that the sole or principal argument which leads him to fix on the year 1472 consists in the words "jam pridem," which describe the printing of Gasparino's letters as having taken place "a long time ago." To this we reply that "jam pridem" signifies "formerly," or "some time ago," and is perfectly applicable to the space of a few months which elapsed between the first and the second issue of Fichet's press.[26] The expression "jam diu" would have been the right one to employ, if a longer period had been intended. Cardinal Bessario used this very phrase in a letter addressed to Fichet the last day of August, 1471, alluding to a letter (to which he had received no answer) sent on the 13th of December, 1470, seven or eight months before.[27]

It is also natural to suppose that a work presenting scholars with the best examples of style should be followed at once by the Orthography, or art of spelling, of the same author as a complementary volume. Moreover, only the Letters are mentioned in the Orthography as having issued from the press. This would hardly have been the case if other books had already appeared.

There is another serious objection to the later date. We know from a letter of Cardinal Bessario to Fichet that towards the end of November, 1471,[28] Gaguin was at Rome. It is contrary to all probability that he was in Paris at the end of the following month, or on the 1st of January, 1472.

The paper employed for printing this book is a strong and very thick paper, of the best quality. The watermarks are the crowned fleur-de-lis in a shield, with the letter J at the end, and a large gothic letter P surmounted by a cross. These marks are exactly the same as in the preceding book.

Shortly afterwards appeared an edition of Sallust, the Latin historian of the conspiracy of Catiline and of the war with

Jugurtha. The date can be easily determined by the following verses, which are placed at the end of the Jugurtha:

> Nunc parat arma virosque simul rex maximus orbis
> Hostibus antiquis exitium minitans.
> Nunc igitur bello studeas gens Pariseorum,
> Cui Martis quondam gloria magna fuit.
> Exempla tibi sint nunc fortia facta virorum,
> Quae digne memorat Crispus in hoc opere.
> Armigeris tuis Alemanos adnumeres qui
> Hos pressere libros, arma futura tibi.

The historical fact alluded to is the preparation for the war declared against Charles, Duke of Burgundy. Consequently the Sallust was printed towards the end of January or the beginning of February, 1471.[29] The last words, "arma futura tibi," show that hostilities had not begun yet. The book was very likely in the hands of the compositors some time before. It forms a quarto volume, divided into two parts: thirty-five leaves for the first part, containing the text of the Catiline, followed by a blank leaf; sixty-eight leaves for the Jugurtha, the last leaf being printed on the *recto* only; altogether 106 leaves, twenty-three lines to the full page.[30]

The copy that belonged to the Sorbonne is printed on vellum, and decorated with handsome painted borders at the beginning of each part, with illuminated initials for each book. It is now exhibited in the show-room of the "Galerie Mazarine" at the Bibliothèque Nationale. At the end, a contemporary hand has written, "*Fichetanus Salustius.*" Philippe observes that this inscription gives support to the idea that Fichet was the principal promoter of the edition.[31]

There are some differences in the title of the copy on vellum as compared with a copy on paper, also in the Bibliothèque Nationale. Some faults are corrected in the press, but, as was noticed by Van Praet,[32] the correction does not extend beyond the first leaf.

Chevillier in his list puts down as the second book printed by our German typographers an edition of Florus with Latin verses by Robert Gaguin at the end.

The distichs of Gaguin are addressed to the readers of Florus: "Robertus Gaguinus Lucei (*sic*) Annei Flori lectoribus salutem optat": and are as follows:

> Quos nulla in terris concluserat ora Quirites
> Haec Flori obstrictos parva tabella capit:
> Et quaeque eximia produxit Livius arte
> Bella, duces, pompas, rite coacta tenet.
> Quo vero exemplo vobis sperare futurum
> Qui fama et quaestu fertis in astra gradum.
> Post tumidos nisus, post saeva pericula sortis,
> Ad manes raptos vos brevis urna teget.

This piece is certainly an allusion to the turbulent and haughty conduct of the Duke of Burgundy, at a time when he was menacing the King of France and threatening to overrun the kingdom with a numerous army; and it surveys the dissensions between the princes and Louis XI. As a matter of fact, the copy of Florus that belonged to Heynlin was bound at the time of its publication with the Sallust. From this circumstance, and from the reference which we find in the verses to the events of the moment, we are of opinion that it may be ranged immediately after the Sallust. The watermark (a crowned fleur-de-lis) seems to show that the book is an early impression, being the same as in the two works of Gasparino; but the type does not look so new as in the *Orthographia*. It consists of ninety leaves (including one blank), twenty-three lines to the full page. The size is quarto.[33]

Next on the list we can place with more certainty the Orations of Cardinal Bessario. In a letter from Rome,[34] Bessario states that on the 14th of December, 1470, he had sent to Fichet the manuscript copy of his *Orationes*. Six weeks after, when communications were on the point of being closed by war, Fichet received the parcel by the hands of the Abbot of S. Corneille.[35] In accordance with the cardinal's request,[36] the work was immediately prepared for press. Printed copies were ready towards the middle of April, as we may infer with certainty from a dedication copy presented on the 23rd of that month to Cardinal Rolin, Bishop of Autun, the generous educator and wealthy benefactor of Fichet.[37] Jehan

Rolin had the highest esteem for Bessario; and it was he who had brought about the acquaintance and friendship between the learned patriarch of Nicaea and the doctor of the Sorbonne. As a grateful acknowledgment, Fichet bestowed the first copy of the work of their common friend on one who had every claim to be so preferred.[38]

Other copies were presented to the king, to the princes of the royal family, to the King of England, to the Duke of Burgundy, to the Duke of Savoy, the Emperor Frederick, and other potentates, as also to the chiefs of monastic orders. The distribution of the copies occupied a whole year. Some were printed on vellum and decorated with paintings, like the copy (now in the Vatican Library) offered to the young King of England, the copy sent to the Emperor (now in the Imperial Library at Vienna), and others.

Special printed letters of dedication, annexed to some of them, show clearly that the book was produced more for private distribution than for sale. Fichet had most of these letters transcribed by a secretary, together with the correspondence that passed between himself and Cardinal Bessario. The letter-book containing these invaluable documents, with autograph annotations by Fichet, is bound in a small quarto volume with the *Orationes* printed at the Sorbonne press. It was formerly in the library of the Cardinal Loménie de Brienne, Archbishop of Sens, a great collector of early books in the last century, and now belongs to the Bibliothèque Nationale.[39]

The printed text of the *Orationes* consists of forty leaves in quarto, containing twenty-three lines to a full page. The dedicatory letters, printed or manuscript, are of course not included in this collation. They differ in each copy according to their length.

For many years Fichet had been teaching the art of eloquence to the students of the University of Paris.[40] The lectures, delivered by him in public, were taken down by his auditors, and some manuscript copies circulated among scholars. As they were generally defective, Fichet prepared a revised text and had it printed at the Sorbonne under his own careful supervision. As each part or chapter of his *Rhetoric* was written, he handed it to the compositors.⁴¹ The work was much improved as it passed through the press; definitions being altered and made clearer by the author in correcting the proof-sheets.⁴²

As soon as a sheet was printed off, a transcript was made on vellum by a copyist and richly illuminated, following the divisions of the printed page exactly, line for line. This splendid copy was presented, previously to the distribution of the printed book, to a prince of the royal blood, Charles, Count of Maine, the greatest lover and collector of books of his time in France, as we learn from the dedicatory epistle. In this masterly piece Fichet extols the noble and glorious passion for books, enumerating the most famed libraries from the earliest antiquity to the present age,⁴³ finally reserving for the prince the most flattering terms of laudatory eloquence. A fine miniature painting represents the author in the costume of a doctor of the Sorbonne, humbly kneeling before the prince and offering him his book. For many years after the invention of printing, it was usual, in obedience to the rules of polite etiquette, to offer such manuscript copies, richly illuminated, of books already in print to sovereigns, princes, and other persons of high rank, in preference to the ordinary printed copies. The manuscript copy of Fichet's *Rhetoric* was presented to Charles, Count of Maine, brother of René, King of Provence, on the 1st of July, 1471, as we know by the date at the end of the dedication. Its present resting-place is the ducal library at Gotha, where it arrived after going through vicissitudes at present unknown to us. " Habent sua fata libelli."

The printed copies were not ready until a fortnight afterwards. Some were printed upon vellum, and decorated with illuminated borders. It is easy to imagine that it took a certain time to get them all bound, and properly illuminated, and also to get separate letters printed and added to the dedication-copies. The manuscript copy might have been finished first of all, and presented at once to the prince, who had his library in Paris. Copies intended for persons at a distance could not be sent immediately; some delay, now necessarily unascertainable, would be occasioned by the difficulties of communication at the time. The space of two weeks between the first and second dedication may perhaps be better attributed to the unsatisfactory state of Fichet's health, due to an illness brought on by incessant labour prosecuted with too great eagerness, as he afterwards declared in a letter to a friend.⁴⁴

The first two printed copies were intended to be presented to Cardinal Rolin and Cardinal Bessario. A third was offered simultaneously to René, King of Provence. Jehan Rolin, Bishop of Autun, was the benefactor and financial provider of Fichet; Bessario had introduced him to literature. We are able to give convincing evidence of this from the copy of the *Rhetoric* addressed to Pope Sixtus IV. In the dedication Fichet begs to be excused for not having presented the book to His Holiness earlier. He explains that he was bound to offer it in the first instance, as their right and legitimate due, to the Cardinal-Bishop of Autun, who provided him with his daily bread, and to the Bishop of Nicaea, who was the first to furnish him with books and literary tastes.

The copy of the *Rhetoric* containing the particulars here given is printed on vellum, and decorated with a splendid full-page miniature, reproduced as the frontispiece to this monograph, showing the author kneeling before the Pope and presenting his book.⁴⁵ On the right side of the papal throne stands, with his long white beard, the first among the surrounding circle of high ecclesiastical dignitaries, Cardinal Bessario, the old friend of Fichet. This highly interesting volume, bound in embroidered silk, is now preserved in the library of the British Museum.

The first printed copy offered to Cardinal Rolin is lost. Fortunately a duplicate proof of the letter of dedication addressed to him has come down to us. It is printed on paper, and is bound up with a set of four other letters, in print⁴⁶ or in manuscript, formerly in the old library of the Sorbonne and now in the Bibliothèque Nationale. [It bears the mark Z. 1683 in the Reserve.] These letters were evidently collected by Fichet, as in the case of Bessario's Orations. The heading of the letter to Jehan Rolin is in red.⁴⁷ Fichet styles himself the pupil (alumnus) of the Bishop of Autun. He says positively, as in the letter to the Pope, that no one had an earlier or better claim to receive a copy of the book than he (Jehan Rolin) who for the last ten years had constantly up to the present day supplied him with liberal funds.

Fichet discharged another debt of grateful acknowledgment by sending a copy of his *Rhetoric* to Guillaume Chartier, Bishop of Paris, who had encouraged and decided him to stay in the city. "Not only," says he, "were you the first of all during my rectorate to reward me with an ecclesiastical benefice (non solum ecclesiastico beneficio quo tempore rectoratum gerebam primus omnium remunerasti), but when I had taken the degree of Doctor it was by your bounty that I remained in Paris (verum etiam sumptis doctoralibus insignibus Parisiis remorandi tuo beneficio causa fuisti)."⁴⁸

The last copy of the *Rhetoric* presented by Fichet was dedicated to Charles of Bourbon, Archbishop of Lyons. The printed letter attached to the copy is on paper; it is dated March 31st, and is followed by part of the letter to Cardinal Bessario, reprinted with its subscription, "scriptum impressumque in ædibus Sorbonæ 1471." Bibliographers have been mistaken in inferring from this that the book was printed towards the end of March, 1471. We are indeed of opinion that it was then in the press, but we are convinced that the book was not finally completed until three months afterwards, and that it was issued only on July 15th. We have already given conclusive evidence of the fact in the letters addressed to Cardinal Rolin and to Pope Sixtus IV. The letter to Cardinal Bessario has no month added to the date, for the reason that when the copy was ready for presentation it remained some time in the hands of Fichet. Owing to the insecurity of the roads at the time he was obliged to wait for an opportunity of sending a safe messenger to Rome; and foreseeing that delay⁴⁹ was unavoidable, and its duration uncertain, omitted to particularize the date.

It was late in the day when Fichet thought of sending his book to Charles of Bourbon. He knew that the archbishop was an intimate friend of Bessario, and offered him the *Rhetoric* as a mark of deference in consideration of the position in which they stood to each other as common friends of Bessario. To show the prelate what terms he was on with the illustrious cardinal he annexed to his present letter of dedication part of the letter of gratitude which he had previously written to Bessario as the patron of his new work, and the instigator of his literary studies.

After this explanation we can easily understand the mistake of Brunet (*Manuel du Libraire*, ii., 242), who, reading only the date 1471 placed at the end of the letter relating to Bessario, ascribed the same date without further reflection to the dedication addressed to Charles of Bourbon. Brunet had also seen at the Bibliothèque Nationale a manuscript copy on vellum of the same two dedicatory epistles joined to a printed copy on paper of the *Rhetoric*, and from this was induced to believe that it was the very copy presented to the Archbishop of Lyons. But elsewhere he states that a similar dedication exists in the copy printed on vellum which formerly belonged to the Duc de la Vallière, and was bought at his sale by the Imperial Library of Vienna. He then concludes from these three copies that the epistles ought to be found in most of the other copies of the edition. Under these circumstances Philippe does not hesitate to say that Fichet placed the *Rhetoric* under the patronage of Charles of Bourbon. This is a gross blunder, as we shall proceed to prove. The copy of the *Rhetoric* on paper, with the printed letter preceding it, in the Reserve (X. 2052) of the Bibliothèque Nationale, is the only one that really belonged to Charles. The first page is finely illuminated in gold and colours, with his arms. The other copy (Réserve X. 1114) was never the property of the archbishop. It belonged to Laurent Bureau, doctor of the Sorbonne, who became confessor to Charles VIII. and Louis XII., and afterwards Bishop of Sisteron. His arms are painted at the beginning of the text, with his device, "Amor meus crucifixus est," at the foot of the page. His initials, L. B. t. (Laurentius Burellus theologus), are also to be found inserted in the first illuminated letter of the text.[60] The manuscript leaves of dedication alluded to are much shorter than the other leaves of the volume, and have evidently been added to it in modern times. Van Praet does not much believe in their genuineness, and he thinks that it is a careful modern imitation of the writing of the time. Philippe is of a different opinion. Our own view is that it is a mere transcription of the printed dedication made by a collector desirous of adding it to his copy, which was perhaps one on vellum. In fact we consider it as a document liable to suspicion, and very likely a forgery. M. L. Delisle, the best judge on the subject, is of our opinion, and has no doubt of the forgery which we suspect.

The two similar leaves mentioned as occurring in the vellum copy from the Gaignat and La Vallière collections, now at Vienna, have the same origin. They are at present missing.[31]

Now that we have cleared up the mystery of the three copies dedicated to Charles of Bourbon, which have puzzled former bibliographers, and conclusively reduced them to a single one, the fact is established that the Archbishop of Lyons was not the patron chosen by the author. This fact will appear much more clearly when we have proved that the real date of the dedication by Fichet is 1472 (New Style), and not 1471, as is generally supposed.

Fichet, as we have seen, kept duplicate copies or proofs of the printed letters of dedication sent with the copies of the *Rhetoric* arranged in order. We have given in a previous note a list of the respective owners of these copies. The name of Charles of Bourbon does not appear either in print or manuscript. In Fichet's copy-book of the letters accompanying the Orations of Bessario, the seventeenth and last letter is addressed to the Dean and Canons of the Church of Lyons (Clarissimis patribus decano singulisque Lugdunsis ecclesie canonicis), and dated from the Sorbonne on the 2nd of April, 1472 (Edibus Sorbone Parisii scriptum quarto Nonas Apriles. Anno secundo et septuagesimo qua . . .). The word is not completed, and the copy-book stops suddenly here.[32] In our opinion the copy of the *Rhetoric* intended for the Archbishop of Lyons was sent by **the same** messenger as the Orations of Bessario;

consequently the former letter, dated exactly two days before the other, must be interpreted as the 31st of March, 1472, the feast of Easter falling that year on the 29th of March. We conclude by two pieces of internal evidence. The types of the letter addressed to Charles of Bourbon look rather heavier and more worn than in the other letters, or in the text of the *Rhetoric*. The copy is distinguished by containing many more pen corrections by the editor than those previously distributed, and one leaf (fo. 37) is reprinted with a definitive text much altered. Moreover, the first copy of such a book presented to a chosen patron ought, according to the rules of politeness, to have been a copy on vellum. After nine months no copy on vellum was left;[53] and a copy on paper, richly illuminated with the arms of Charles of Bourbon, was offered by Fichet instead.

The *Rhetoric* forms a thick quarto volume of 194 leaves, including three leaves blank.[54] The printed or manuscript letters added to some copies are not included in this collation. The number of lines is twenty-three, and in some cases twenty-four, as in leaves 72, 73, and 74. The text ends on the recto of leaf 192. On the 192nd leaf follows a panegyric on **the author**, in fourteen distichs, or twenty-eight Latin verses by Robert Gaguin. The same piece had appeared six months before in the *Orthographia*, but in the present reprint some verses were added, in which Savoy is expressly mentioned as the native country of Fichet, who is to be the perpetual glory of France :

> Felix illa quidem tali Sabaudia alumno
> Cujus erit Gallis perpetuatus honor.

After Fichet's *Rhetoric* we are not aware of any other dated book of the year 1471, except a folio edition of the *Elegantiae Linguae Latinae*, by Laurentius Valla. The text was at the request of Heynlin revised by Pierre Paul Vieillot (Senilis), secretary to the King of France. Heynlin also divided the text into chapters, and compiled a vocabulary of the most important expressions, followed by a letter of acknowledgment to his friend, who had fulfilled the duty of clearing the text from the faults and spurious readings of the copyists. The Valla is the most important work so far produced at the Sorbonne. It forms a thick folio volume of 262 leaves, including four blank leaves. It is arranged in twenty-seven quires, mostly of ten, but some of eight leaves. The number of lines is thirty-two to a full page.[55] The type begins to appear rather worn when compared with the preceding books.

Two other volumes were printed at the Sorbonne Press a little before the Valla, an edition of Cicero's *Orator*, and a *Valerius Maximus*. No copy of them has ever been found, but of their existence there can be no doubt. They are mentioned, together with the Valla, in a letter of Heynlin, as impressions already issued some time ago from the same press. Fichet had left Paris just then in order to proceed to the king's court. He was intrusted by Cardinal Bessario with the duty of expounding to his majesty a plan of general pacification, and of determining Louis XI. to undertake the crusade against the Turks, who were then the great danger that threatened Christianity. During the time that Fichet had to wait before he could be admitted to an audience with the king, several works of Cicero, brought over to Tours by certain booksellers or printers,[56] fell by chance into his hands. In the midst of the noise of the court he derived great profit from reading them, and more pleasure than when he had read them often and often again at home.[57] It would have been more pleasant still if each book had been better corrected and divided into chapters like the *Orator* of Cicero, the *Valerius Maximus*, and the *Laurentius Valla*, already printed under the care of Heynlin.[58] Fichet accordingly gives instructions to his friend concerning an edition of the *De Officiis* and other works of Cicero which the Paris printers were preparing for the press, telling him to improve it by applying to it his method of accurate correction and careful division into chapters.[59]

These particulars are given by Fichet in his letter dated from the house of Raoul Toustain, his host, at Tours, the 7th March, 1472 (1471, Old Style), and printed as a preface at the head of the edition of Cicero's *Offices* and other tracts (*De Amicitia, De*

Senectute, *Somnium Scipionis*, and *Paradoxa*) printed with the Sorbonne type.

From this document it appears clearly that three books, the *Orator* of Cicero, *Valerius Maximus*, and *Laurentius Valla*, were successively printed under the care of Johann Heynlin, alias de la Pierre, before March, 1472, that is, during the last month of 1471, after Fichet's *Rhetoric*. The manuscript copy of the *Offices* and other works of the Latin philosopher had been for some time (at least as early as the first two months of 1472) in the hands of the compositors, and the work was so much advanced that printed copies could be issued and sold in the last days of this very month of March, 1472.[60] The volume is a folio like the Valla, and consists of 124 leaves, including one blank. A full page contains thirty-one lines. Heynlin offered a copy to George of Baden, Bishop of Metz, and accompanied it with a special letter printed on vellum, and finely illuminated with the arms of the prelate in gold and colours. At the end of the letter, after the usual complimentary form, "Vale," he added in his own handwriting the words, "Prestantissime pater."[61]

Next in date we must place here the *Speculum Vitae Humanae* by Roderic, Bishop of Zamora, a folio volume (142 leaves, including one blank, thirty-two lines to a page), commonly classified by bibliographers among the latest productions of the Sorbonne press. The copy preserved in the British Museum (C. 13. b. 9), however, possesses three supplementary leaves, not found in any other example, and these contain dedicatory letters from the printers, hitherto unpublished and unknown, one of which, as we shall see, is dated April 22nd, 1472. On account of the importance of these letters they are printed verbatim at the end of this monograph, and a page from one of them is given in facsimile. Nevertheless, we must here briefly indicate their contents.

The first of the three letters is styled by the rubricator *Epistola comendatoria*, and is directed to John II., Duke of Bourbon and Auvergne, peer and chamberlain of France. A visit which, during a stay in Paris, this high personage had paid, of his own accord, to the humble rooms of the printers to see their printing formes and presses is mentioned as a mark of interest and honour, stimulating them to fresh alacrity. In their gratitude they offer, as a little present, profitable, and, as they hope, agreeable to the duke, the *Mirror of Human Life*, composed by Roderic, Bishop of Zamora, lately published at Rome, and now reprinted by their industry.

The second letter, entitled *Epistola recommendatoria*, is addressed to Robert de Estouteville, Provost of Paris, whom the printers thank most heartily for the excellent treatment they had already received in this city of Paris, where they are treated not as mere guests and newcomers, but as freemen and citizens. The *Mirror of Human Life*, they say, lately published at Rome, we have but just finished printing at Paris for the public benefit, and especially for your sake, as we know that you will gladly read of the manners and different conditions of men which this work reviews. The letter ends with this distich, in the style of those of Fichet, offering the book:

> Que tua pietas conservat, clare Roberte,
> Suscipiat munus quod tibi sit placitum.

The third and last letter is addressed to the King of France, and contains, like the previous ones, a grateful acknowledgment of the kindness received by the printers in Paris, the capital of the kingdom, " where we are so well treated that no more delightful freedom is possible for us, who in reliance only on your clemency greatly desire that the books we print should render illustrious the kingdom made happy by your reign." Alluding slightly to the quarrel with the Duke of Burgundy they appeal to the royal magnanimity for peace and conciliation. With the utmost reverence they present to his majesty, for the government of his subjects and as a token of their loyalty, the *Mirror of Human Life*, as they have fashioned, *i.e.* printed it, with their own hands. This letter to Louis XI. is dated and inscribed, " Tua in Lutetia, **x. Kal.** Maii anni millesimi quadringentesimi secundi supra septuagesimum manibus tibi deditissimorum Martini, Udalrici atque Michaelis impressum."

The 10th of the Kalends of May corresponds to April 22nd, 1472, one month after the departure of Fichet from the court at Amboise. Although the name of Fichet does not appear in the letter, we are of opinion that it was suggested, if not written by him, in pursuance of his scheme of pacification.

It will be observed that the names of the printers are not in the same order as that in which they are given in previous books of their printing. In the first book (*Gasparini Epistolae*) they appear as Michael, Martinus, and Udalricus; in the second (*Gasparini Orthographia*) as Udalricus, Martinus, and Michael; here as Martinus, Udalricus, and Michael; and in a fourth book (*Epistolae Cynicae*), to be mentioned hereafter, in the same order as in the first. These changes in the order of the names seems to have arisen from a mutual deference, and may be observed throughout their partnership.

The Cicero *De Officiis* is the last book in which the name of Heynlin appears as corrector or editor. It was followed by an edition of the *Tusculanae Quaestiones*, printed in the same size and with the same types, and with the same method of division by chapters. Copies are sometimes bound with the *De Officiis*, but they evidently form two distinct publications issued independently. Brunet and other bibliographers are mistaken when they describe them as forming the two parts of a single complete volume.[62] At the end of the *Tusculans* we read seven distichs of Erhard Windsberg, who seems to have succeeded to Heynlin as corrector or reviser in the printing office of the Sorbonne. The last three distichs mention the division of the book into chapters, and praise the skill displayed by the printers.[63] The book forms a folio volume of eighty-eight leaves, including one blank. A full page contains thirty-one lines, as in the *De Officiis*.[64]

Next in order after these works of Cicero and the *Speculum Vitae Humanae*, we think that we can place the Letters of Plato, translated into Latin by Leonardo Bruni of Arezzo. The publication of them was suggested to Fichet by reading the work of Bessario on the Philosophy of Plato. In a letter of the 4th April,

1472, from the Sorbonne, Fichet writes to his friend : "I was possessed by such eagerness to read your book just received, that through the nights of this Eastertide I sought in vain a way to sleep." Plato," he says, "kept my attention fixed in admiration of lovely things which I had never read before."[65b] He is so charmed and excited that he solicits a special favour from Bessario. It is that he would write a preface addressed to the School of Paris. "In this preface," says Fichet, "you must enjoin me to present your beloved Plato in your name to our Paris students, and give everyone the opportunity of making a copy of him.[66] Finish this preface with all speed that I may present your Plato in your name to the School of Paris as soon as it assembles after this Easter vacation.[67] Funds shall be provided, and I need not say I will exert myself that in the meantime our printers may strike off many Platos from the Plato you have sent me." From the lines just quoted we see something of the relation between Fichet, the real owner of the Sorbonne press, and the printers. Fichet had to pay the cost of printing some time after the work was finished, deducting sums received by the printers for copies sold in the meantime.

For this intended edition of Plato Fichet speaks of some copies to be printed on vellum if he can afford the expense, as had been done for Bessario's Orations. He will place them in the public libraries of the colleges of Paris, that they may be read to the remotest ages.[68] Exactly one month afterwards, on the 4th May, 1472, the University, assembled at the Convent of the Mathurins, addressed an official letter of acknowledgment to Cardinal Bessario for the presentation made to them by Fichet of his work on Plato, and also for a copy of his Orations.[69]

Full of enthusiasm for divine Plato, and impatient to spread his teaching, our doctor of the Sorbonne gave immediate orders to his copyists[70] for a manuscript of the Letters of Plato translated into Latin. This charming copy, written on vellum, a little volume of the size of a pocket-book,[71] was offered to a friend of his, Jehan Choard of Buzenval, late Provost-Lieutenant of Paris, member of the

Assembly of Notables held at Tours in 1470, and at the present time Chancellor to the Duke of Calabria, brother of King René of Provence. It was preceded by a letter of presentation dated from the Sorbonne on the 27th April, twenty-three days after the letter addressed to Bessario. The book, however, was not presented till a fortnight afterwards, as we learn from another letter to the same person, also written by Fichet, inserted in front of the volume, and dated the 13th May.

Printed copies of these Letters of Plato followed, we think, not very long after. We presume their number was limited, as we can trace only three copies. One is mentioned in the catalogue of the Crevenna Library, sold by auction at Amsterdam at the end of the eighteenth century, but it is not known where it is now preserved. The other belonged to Heynlin, and is preserved with his other books in the University Library at Basel. A third exists in the public library at Angers, bound with the Epistles of Phalaris, Brutus and Crates and the Florus. Neither of them contains Fichet's letters found in the manuscript copy. The printed volume, a quarto, consists altogether of fifty leaves.[72] A full page averages twenty-three lines; the last page contains only fourteen lines, and beneath them is the following distich by Fichet:

> Discite rectores divinitus ore Platonis
> Quid vos, quod cives reddat in urbe bonos.

Bessario did not send the prefatory letter solicited by Fichet. Probably he was prevented by sickness or some other cause unknown from complying with the request of his friend, and the Letters of Plato took the place of his work. We are pretty sure that no vellum copies were made of Plato's Epistles. Had it been so, they should have been found in the libraries of the Parisian colleges to which the publisher would have given them, as he expressed his intention of doing if they had ever been printed.

At this time Fichet was occupied with philosophical ideas and studies. We are strongly of opinion that simultaneously or after the Letters of Plato he resolved to publish the letters of other Greek philosophers. The Letters of Phalaris, translated into Latin, were sent to press in one volume with the Letters of Brutus and Crates. At the head of the Letters of Crates, disciple of Diogenes the Cynic, we read before the preface the following verses:

> Hae tibi virtutum stimulos et semina laudum
> Atque exempla dabunt Cynicae, o lector studiose.

(Studious reader, these cynic letters will incite to virtue and sow the seed and set the example of meritorious deeds.)

On the reverse of the last leaf we find a piece of eight verses:

> Erhardi Vuinsberg epigramma ad Germanos librarios egregios Michaelem, Martinum atque Udalricum.
>
> Plura licet summae dederis Alemania laudi
> At reor hoc majus te genuisse nihil,
> Quod prope divinam summa ex industria fingis
> Scribendi hanc artem, multiplicans studia.
> Foelices igitur Michael, Martineque semper
> Vivite et Ulrice hoc queis opus imprimitur.
> Erhardum vestrum et non dedignemini amore,
> Cui fido semper pectore clausi eritis."

Erhard Windsberg, whose name appears for the first time in a distich at the end of Cicero's *Tusculans*, as we have already remarked, seems to have assumed the functions of Johann Heynlin when he was prevented by absence, or some other cause unknown to us, from continuing to revise the texts printed at the Sorbonne. As we have noticed, there is no further trace of Heynlin's literary collaboration after March, 1472. Erhard was no doubt a friend of our printers, a German, it may be, a native of the same country. Chevillier says that he was a student in medicine," and also a friend of Heynlin. He afterwards returned to Germany, and from a letter written by him from Saxony in 1486 to Reuchlin, we learn that he became doctor in medicine. The copy of the Letters of Phalaris, Brutus, and Crates, given to him by Fichet, is to be seen in the Cantonal Library of Lucerne. It contains autograph notes of Fichet in the margins, and an inscription on the fly-leaf and cover in his handwriting: "Per me M. Erhardo

Ventimontano (*i.e.*, Windsberg), teste meo signo manuali," and, below, the mark of Fichet, a Greek Φ.

Most bibliographers have assigned to these Letters an early place among the impressions of the Sorbonne. But the admiration expressed in the verses of Erhard, and the tribute of praise bestowed on his friends the printers, do not prove at all that the volume is one of the first productions of that press. It merely shows that Erhard felt a natural emotion of wondering enthusiasm when he was allowed to penetrate to the printing-room of the establishment, and was initiated into the mystery of the new mechanical art of writing and multiplying copies of books for scholars. The comparative heaviness of the type proves from internal evidence that these Letters were not printed so early as has been generally supposed. The collection forms a quarto volume of eighty-two leaves, with twenty-three lines to a full page.[75]

We are aware of the existence of two other impressions executed at the Sorbonne in 1471-72, but neither of them bears a date, and we confess that we have not yet found sufficient evidence to assign one to them with certainty. One of them, *Augustini Dathi Senensis isagogicus libellus in eloquentiæ precepta*, we are inclined to place between the *Rhetoric* of Fichet and the *Orator* of Cicero on account of the similarity of the subject. It is divided into chapters like the latter, according to the method recommended by Fichet to Heynlin. The unique copy of this edition, unknown to Panzer, Hain, Brunet, and other bibliographers, was mentioned for the first time by Philippe, who gives an accurate description of the book and a facsimile of the first page.[76] This copy, which was Heynlin's own, and which is bound with a MS. of Cicero's *Rhetoric*, is now preserved in the University Library at Basel. The *Dathus* is a small quarto of forty-six leaves, including two blanks at the end, with twenty-three lines to a full page.

The other undated book is a Virgil. After the Latin prose writers, the editors of the Sorbonne turned their attention to classical poetry. We believe that the edition of Virgil's *Ecloges* was the first work printed in this branch of literature. There is no preface. The following verses, indicative of the nature of the contents, are placed after a title in two lines at the head of the first page:

> Hic deflet Melibœus profugiat quid inique,
> Tityrus ast lætus quis contulit otia dicit.

The book ends with a single line for the colophon: "Finis foelix Georgicorum Virgilii." The volume, a small folio, contains fifty leaves, including a blank at the beginning, with thirty-two lines to a page, like the Valla. The only copy known to exist is in the possession of Mrs. Rylands of Manchester. It is exactly described by Philippe, who gives a facsimile of the first and last pages.[77]

We again find the name of Erhard Windsberg in a folio edition of Juvenal and Persius, printed a short time after the Letters of Phalaris. Like the *Rhetoric* and the Letters of Plato, it was preceded by a MS. copy prepared for a high personage, Peter Doriolle, Chancellor of France. On the first page a fine miniature painting represents the chancellor seated at a table, with seals and implements for writing. About him officials and clerks are busy despatching and sealing letters and other State documents. On the left is seen a humble personage kneeling, with his head uncovered; he is accompanied by a young boy with his hands clasped in an attitude of supplication, and presents to the chancellor the MS. of Juvenal. This illumination is followed by a dedicatory poem in thirty-two verses, which form an acrostic: PIERRE DORIOLLE CHANCELIER DE FRANCE.[78] The volume, a small folio, neatly written on choice vellum, is finely executed. At the beginning of the satires there are initial letters illuminated and historiated with personages suggested by the subject of the poem. At the end stands an address by Erhard in two verses as follows:

> ERHARDUS D. J. JUVENALIS CULTORI" F[ELICITATEM] OPTAT.
>
> Ecce parens Satyrarum princeps Eliconis et auctor
> In pravos mittens tela severa notae.
>
> To the lovers of Juvenal Erhard wishes happiness.

See the father of Satire, a chief writer of Helicon, hurling upon the wicked the piercing darts of ignominy.

The text of the manuscript is accompanied with notes and an interlinear commentary, written in a smaller character, but by the same hand. The notes and the commentary are probably due to Erhard.[80]

In the printed book, published evidently after the written copy, there are no notes and no commentary; but to the text of Juvenal are added the Satires of Persius. The Juvenal ends on leaf sixty-one verso, with the same distich of Erhard as in the manuscript copy. The Persius begins immediately after, on leaf sixty-two recto, and ends on the seventy-third leaf with another poetical piece composed by Erhard, to extol, much in the same way as in the edition of Phalaris, Brutus, and Crates, the new invention of printing and those who exercised it:

ERHARDI TETRASTICHON AD GERMANOS LIBRARIOS INGENUOS.

Ecce tibi princeps satyrarum codice parvo
Persiius (*sic*) arte nova impressus et ingenio.
Foelices igitur Alemannos arte magistra
Qui studia ornantes fertis in astra gradus.

Tetrastich of Erhard to the noble German stationers.

Here you have the prince of satirists, Persius, printed in a small volume by a new and ingenious art. Happy then are you Germans who, by this sovereign art advancing our studies, tread the path leading to the skies.

Peter Doriolle was appointed chancellor June 26th, 1472. The manuscript copy of Juvenal was presented to him shortly after he entered upon his duties, something like six weeks or two months, the space of time necessary for it to be written and illuminated by the excellent scribes (egregii scriptores) of the Sorbonne. The printed copies, completed by the addition of the text of Persius, were issued soon after, probably towards the end of August, or in September, 1472. Philippe remarked that the type used in the book was rather worn, and hence conjectured that it appeared towards the middle of the year. The reasons already given justify us in placing it some months later.

The book forms a small folio volume of seventy-four leaves

(including two blank leaves), a full page containing on an average thirty-two lines, as in the Virgil.

Four copies of this edition are known. One, which belonged to Heynlin, is now at Basel. Two are in England: one in the library of Magdalen College, Oxford; the other in **Mrs. Rylands' library at Manchester.** The fourth copy exists in **the public library at Avignon.** Some copies present slight **differences**; but the number of leaves and the number of lines agree, and the edition is the same. We have already remarked that corrections and alterations were made in some of the books printed at the Sorbonne while they were passing through the press, and bibliographers have noticed the same corrections made with a pen in certain copies of the printed texts.

We must now retrace our steps. Since the outbreak of hostilities between the King of France and the Duke of Burgundy, Fichet's one desire had been to make peace between them, and to reconcile Louis XI. with his other enemies and rivals, on the lines recommended and urged by Cardinal Bessario. A truce, renewable at will, had been concluded between the contending parties on April 4, 1471. The cardinal's scheme was to persuade the king, the duke, the princes, and the rest to put aside their quarrels, **and to** sink them in a common effort with the Pope and all **the** potentates **of** Christendom for a general crusade against the Turks.

In accordance with this plan, the *Orationes*, or addresses to the Italian princes, eloquently showing the necessity of relieving Europe from the pressing danger of invasion by the Turks, were printed at the Sorbonne press under Fichet's supervision, and at his own expense. With unselfish devotion he gave himself entirely to this noble cause.[n] Special or general letters, printed or written by him, were appended to each of the copies sent to the persons whom **it was** intended to address. More than a year was employed in the preparation and distribution of the copies, which had to be sent to their various destinations in France, Germany, England, Italy, and even Spain. Communications were difficult, the roads were insecure at that time, and it was often necessary to wait weeks or months for an opportunity of forwarding a copy.

Although the printed letter to the king and the French princes collectively appealing for a reconciliation bears the date of August 5, 1471,[81b] the copy specially designed for Louis XI. was not presented at that time.

In order to open the way for conciliation, Fichet endeavoured first to secure support for Bessario's pacific scheme of terminating the civil war in France to the common advantage of Christendom. Almost all who had received his letters accompanying the work of Bessario expressed approval, and offered sums of money as contributions to the Crusade. He nobly declined their offers,[82] accepting only from the provincial minister of the Minims a letter of participation in the good works of the friars and nuns of the order. Enclosed in a little bag he received it with reverence, and valued it above the treasures of any king.[83]

Forty-six copies of Bessario's discourses had been distributed gratuitously in all parts of France and Germany,[84] when Fichet solicited an audience, that he might present a copy in person to the king. This was not a printed copy, but one elegantly written on vellum, and illuminated as beautifully as possible, with a portrait of his majesty at the beginning delicately painted in miniature, and below it a dedicatory couplet.

Fichet was in the hall of the royal residence at Amboise, near Tours, on March 6, 1472; and on the 21st of that month he writes to his friend. In this letter he gives the following particulars of his reception by the king:

"Orationes tuas quam apparatissimas potui reddidi Serenissimo Regi, verbaque feci paucis cum de concordia christianis principibus inter se necessaria tum de bello contra Crucis hostes obeundo; nihilque praetermisi quod tuo nomine regi esset offerendum. Gracioso quidem vultu librum tuum excepit, legitque parumper prefatiunculam quam operi tuo prescripsi. Revolutis dein membranis, picturas et imagines in marginibus sparsas cominus inspexit. Tum glosulas in oratione Demosthenis a te quidem positas fere singulas legit.

Erant enim auro varioque colore in contextu orationis interjectae.
Inter legendum questiunculas a me quasdam rogavit quibus presto fuit
responsum. Postremo reversus ad codicis principium disticon ter
quaterque resumpsit quod in calce regie imaginis scriptum repperit :

> Fausta futura tibi Rex accipe Bessarionis
> Munera quae prosint et foris et domi.

A secretis qui aderat, librum custodiendum excepit. Rex tue
paternitati tandem pro munere gracias egit; de domestica vero
concordia belloque foris ne verbum quidem unum fecit."[84b]

Fichet then in the most pathetic terms implores the cardinal to
make haste, the ground being well prepared, and to come to France
as papal legate. He swears solemnly before Christ that he will
never desert his friend, whether alive and in danger, or dead.
"Arise," he says, "expected hope of France ! Arise !" (Exsurge
tandem, exspectatio Galliarum ! exsurge !)

During the time that he was obliged to be absent on his mission
at court, Fichet, as we have already noticed, sent instructions to his
friend Heynlin to print the *Offices* of Cicero ; and in his letter,
dated March 7, 1472, he mentions the *Orator*, the *Valerius
Maximus*, and the *Valla*, as having been issued some time before.
Immediately after the 21st of that month he returned to the
Sorbonne;[85] and we find him here at home indulging himself
during the Easter holidays in his favourite occupation of reading
Plato.

In his letter of the 4th of April, written from the Sorbonne,
Fichet appeals to Bessario as urgently and as eloquently as he had
done a fortnight before; and at last the cardinal decided, for the
sake of restoring peace, and, as he hoped, saving Christendom, to
undertake the long journey.

Old and infirm, he left Rome, and travelling by easy stages
passed the Alps. He had to wait more than a month for a safe-
conduct from the king to enable him to pursue his way. On the
15th of August he reached Saumur. He immediately advised the
king of his arrival. A few days later, accompanied by Fichet, he

was received in audience by the monarch, and laid before him, besides some other matters, his scheme for the pacification of France. Louis listened while he spoke of certain ecclesiastical matters that were at issue between the courts of France and Rome; a basis was laid down for a future understanding, and the principal points of an agreement were sketched and approved. But when Bessario came to the delicate question of the French princes and the Turkish Crusade, he would not hear of it; and when the cardinal insisted, he looked displeased, and ended by bringing the audience to an abrupt termination. Some historians report that the king made a disrespectful jest on the long patriarchal beard of the legate, that he looked angry, and formally forbade him to stop in France in order to visit the Duke of Brittany and the Duke of Burgundy, as he had intended to do.

Bessario, heart-broken, and accompanied by his friend Fichet, who, as we have seen above, had sworn never to leave him, left the court in the first days of September to return home. On the 13th of that month he reached Lyons, and informed Sixtus IV. of the ill-success of his mission. The king's orders had prevented him from seeing the Duke of Burgundy, and he was on his way back to Rome.

Weary and disheartened, he repassed the Mont Cenis with great difficulty, and fell seriously ill on the other side of the Alps, at Turin. Unable to bear the fatigue of a further journey by land, he embarked on the River Po, and landed at Ravenna, where he died, the 18th of November, 1472.

Fichet arrived alone at Rome a few days after the death of his friend. The Pope received him kindly, and immediately attached him to his person, appointing him to be his chamberlain. He also made him a present of a handsome church revenue, valued at 500 Roman pounds. Weary of French politics, Fichet never returned to the city which owed so much to his wisdom and enterprise.

He wrote from Rome to advise his colleagues of his new position.[86] At the assembly held at the College of the Mathurins on December 5, 1472, the Congregation of the Sorbonne sent a letter of acknowledgment to the Pope for the great honour bestowed upon one of their most eminent members.

The departure of Fichet from the Sorbonne had been so sudden that he left nearly all his books and his manuscripts there.[85] One of his intimate friends, Jehan Royer (Roerius), who had succeeded Heynlin as prior in 1471, and was afterwards librarian in 1472, continued to keep the printer's work-room in the library buildings until Easter, 1473, the date when he resigned his office.

Jehan Royer was the only person who kept up a regular correspondence with Fichet. He was commissioned by Fichet to arrange his affairs, and especially his engagements with the printers.[87]

After Fichet's departure, the printers seem to have been left to go their own way. The Terence, issued after the Juvenal and Persius, is printed in a careless manner; the text is printed like prose, the divisions of the verses not being marked; the acts are not clearly divided; the names of the actors are indicated only by initials placed in the middle of the lines. This defective arrangement is quite unlike the high literary standard of the former editors and correctors. The book is a small folio of eighty-six leaves, with thirty-two lines to a page, like the Juvenal and the Virgil, and is printed with the usual types, but much worn, as Philippe observes. Only two perfect copies of this edition are known: one is Heynlin's copy, and is bound with the Juvenal and Persius; the other is at Manchester, in the John Rylands Library. The copy at the Bibliothèque Nationale is imperfect,[88] wanting the first comedy, the *Andria*.

During the six months that preceded their departure from the Sorbonne in the middle of April, 1473, the printers issued rapidly many books that were likely to find a ready sale, such as the moral tracts of Aeneas Sylvius (Pope Pius II.), *De duobus amantibus*, and *De miseriis curialium*, two small quarto volumes of forty-six and thirty-six leaves, twenty-three lines to the page. Copies of both are in the Bibliothèque Nationale and also in the Mazarine Library. Abandoning classical literature, they entered upon a new line, publishing henceforward theological works. They printed two thick folio volumes of moral theology, viz., Ambrosius, *De Officiis*, with the tract *De Virtutibus*, wrongly attributed to Seneca (ninety-four leaves, thirty-one lines to a page); and Jacobus Magni, *Sophologium* (two hundred and eighteen leaves, including one blank, thirty-two lines to a page). The type of the *Sophologium* is very much worn, as Philippe has observed, and it was probably the last volume issued from the Sorbonne press. These two books must have been printed in much larger numbers than those that preceded them, as many copies are known to exist in libraries in France, in England, and elsewhere. The printers had trained apprentices and workmen, and could produce more speedily than before.

When they removed their presses from the Sorbonne, they settled on their own account in a house in the " grant rue St. Jacques," near the church of St. Benoit, at the sign of " The Golden Sun." The round type which they had cut and cast in imitation of the Roman editions by desire of their introducer, Heynlin, was much worn and almost unfit for use. They engraved a new type of heavier face, in the Gothic style, more able to resist the *blow of the press* upon the hard thick paper generally used.

On the 21st of May, 1473, appeared the *Manipulus Curatorum*, by Guy de Montrocher, the first book executed with the new fount. The first type had disappeared, and the letters had been melted down.

Thus ended the first press established in France, a private press for the benefit of public studies.

NOTES.

NOTES.

(1) *Annals of Parisian Typography, containing an account of the earliest typographical establishments of Paris and notices and illustrations of the most remarkable productions of the Parisian gothic press, compiled principally to shew its general character and its particular influence upon the early English press*, by the Rev. William Parr Greswell; London, MDCCCXVIII. 8vo, with a portrait, engraved on wood, of Ulrich Gering, one of the first Parisian printers; copied from one of the very rare uncancelled copies of La Caille's *Histoire de l'Imprimerie et de la Librairie*, published in 1689.

(2) A surname given from his birthplace, Stein (in French *La Pierre*), a village near Borxheim and Bretten in the Grand Duchy of Baden, in the diocese of Speyer (*Spirensis dioecsis*).

(3) Heynlin had been a student at the University of Leipzig in 1452; in 1459 he was already in Paris, regent of arts in the College of Burgundy. On the 18th of June, 1462, he was made a fellow (*socius*) of the Sorbonne. In 1463 he left France, and kept a term at the University of Basel, where he proceeded M.A. in the following year (1464) under the rectorate of John Blicherod von Gotha. He is inscribed in the Matriculation book (vol. i., p. 17 recto): "Magister Johannes Heynlin de Lapide Sacrae Theologiae Baccalarius," and there is a subsequent mention of his serving as Dean (*Matricula studiosorum*, vol. i., p. 181).

Heynlin returned to France in 1467, and on the 28th of March was elected **Prior of** the Sorbonne. A month after, he gave up his office on account of the weakness of his eyes (see below, note 8), as stated in the register of the Priors (fol. 58). In the **same** year he was raised to the dignity of Rector of the University of Paris. On **the** 25th of March, 1470 (new style), Heynlin was for the second time elected Prior **of** the Sorbonne.

(3b) See *Greswell*, p. 51.

(4) "Michahel de Columbaria" was eighteenth on the list at the spring examinations in 1463, under the decanate of Conrad Jacobi (*Matricula studiosorum*, vol. i., fol. 178). His name is also mentioned in 1461 as a *baccalarius* under the decanate of Peter Zern Lust (fol. 9 verso, 22nd name). He paid a fee of vi.s.

(5) Several bibliographers have suggested that Gering had been a student of the University of Basel. An examination of the Matriculation book shows that in 1461 a student named Udalricus *Gernud* or *Gerund* " de Berona " was examined as a bachelor at the same time as Michael Freyburger (fol. 9 verso), and we find also entries in 1460 of a Nicolaus *Gering*, alias Blairenstein, chaplain of the cathedral of Basel (fol. 5), in 1467 of a Heinricus *Gering* "de Wutterangen, Constant. dyocesis" (fol. 72 verso), and in 1496 of an Udalricus *Guerning* " de Thun, Constantiensis dyocesis " (fol. 99). From these entries it seems clear that the name *Gering* was a familiar one and not likely to be miswritten Gernud or Gerund. In fact Ulrich Gering can hardly have been a graduate of the Basel University, since in the letters of hospitalization granted to him many years after by the Sorbonne (see *Chevillier*, p. 87) he is spoken of only as an "écolier étudiant en l'Université de Paris." If he had been a graduate of any university it must have been mentioned in this document or in the notarial instrument quoted by Chevillier.

Gering could not have learned his art at Berona, *i.e.* Beromünster in Aargau, since printing did not begin there until 1470, by which time, if not earlier, he was already working at Paris. We are strongly of opinion that he was a native of Constanz in Baden (*Constantiensis*), as stated in the colophon of one of his books (see Panzer, ii., p. 307, No. 331). In the postscript of a letter written by Hans Blumenstock, alias Heydelberg, to Hans Amerbach, the celebrated printer at Basel, dated from Paris on the Friday after the feast of St. Bartholomew, 1501, he is called : " Meister *Ulrich Gering*, impressor librorum Parisius von *Costencz* " (see Oskar Hase, *Die Koberger;* Leipzig, 1885, 8vo, p. xliv). Blumenstock, who was Amerbach's agent in Paris, had numerous opportunities of becoming acquainted with Gering, and knew well that he was not of Beromünster, but of Constanz. " Heinricus Gering, de Wutterangen " and " Udalricus Guerning de Thun," of the diocese of Constanz, were probably relations belonging to the family of our printer, as perhaps was also the chaplain Nicolas Gering, who had in his possession a copy of Rodericus Zamorensis, *Speculum Vitae humanae*, one of the books printed at the Sorbonne by Ulrich Gering and his companions (see Philippe, *Origine de l'Imprimerie à Paris;* Paris, 1885, 8vo, p. 218).

(6) Some think that Martin Crantz was the son of the Strasburg workman who was a witness in Gutenberg's last lawsuit with his partner Fust at Mainz in 1455, but we have no evidence of this relationship. We presume rather that he was a countryman of Heynlin, and a native of the same village of Stein. In 1461, we find at Basel a bachelor " Gabriel *Krantz*, de Stein " (*Matricula studiosorum*, fol. 9) entered at the same time as Michael Freyburger, but we cannot ascertain at present whether he belongs to the family of our printer or not.

(7) See Madden, *Lettres d'un Bibliographe;* Paris, 1878 (5th Series), 8vo, p. 156. This author also gives a plan of the ancient building of the Sorbonne, showing the spot occupied by the premises where he places the printing establishment.

(8) We have already mentioned the fact that soon after his first election as prior in 1467, Heynlin excused himself and begged to be discharged of his office on account of an infirmity of the eyes. We give here the text of the passage from the register of the Priors: " Proposuit Prior in aula quom per magnum tempus passus fuisset infirmitatem

oculorum et singulis constabat quod ipse studio vacare non potuisset, quom etiam timeret quod in brevi se studio occupare non auderet secundum quod officium requireret et ideo supplicavit. . . ."

(9) Heynlin already possessed some books of the very early press of Mainz, and also editions of the classics and other works printed at Rome. His private library, consisting of 283 volumes, was after his death bequeathed to the Carthusian house of Klein Basel, on the opposite side of the Rhine, and after the suppression of the said convent passed into the library of the University, where they are now preserved with the original catalogue.

(10) See Philippe, J., *Guillaume Fichet, sa vie et ses œuvres*; Annecy, 1892, 8vo, p. 47: and Moufflet, S., *Etude sur une négociation diplomatique de Louis XI.*; Marseille, 1884, 8vo, pp. 170, 171.

(11) See Philippe, *Guil. Fichet*, p. 56. This author says *Anet* in Eure et Loir. It is a mistake. There was no ecclesiastical benefice at Anet.

(12) "Sumptus amplissimos abhinc decennium ad hunc usque diem continuo suppeditasti" (dedication letter of Fichet's *Rhetoric* [1471] to Rolin, Bibl. Nationale, Réserve, Z. 1683, 4to).

(13) Chevillier says positively that the Society of Sorbonne was at all times poor, and often, in urgent necessity, obliged to borrow money from friends. On nearly all the manuscript books of their library the following inscription was written: " Hic liber est pauperum Magistrorum de Sorbona" (Chevillier, p. 84).

(14) The registers of deliberations and accounts of the Sorbonne have been carefully examined by Franklin, Philippe, and other historians. Not a line, not a word, has been found alluding to the subject. It is evident that the Sorbonne did not spend a farthing on the printers, but allowed them only a temporary hospitality, under the responsibility of the prior and the librarian.

(15) Fichet was born on the 16th of September, 1433, at the Petit Bornand in Savoy, in the diocese of Geneva (see Philippe, *Guillaume Fichet*, pp. 11, 12). He calls himself "Alnetanus" on account of the ecclesiastical benefice of Aunay granted to him; but he signs himself in a letter to the Duke of Savoy " Guillelmus Fichetus, Parisiensis theologus doctor, patria vero Sabaudus." In 1455, he was studying at Avignon, and settled afterwards in Paris.

(16) Copies of the first book printed at Paris are in the British Museum and in the Spencer-Rylands Library.

(17) "Ut qui cum laude et gloria Sorbonico certamini dux praefuisti."

(18) If we reckon the arrival of Freyburger, Gering, and Crantz as occurring quite at the end of 1469, or in the first months of 1470 (new style), there was not too much time to construct the press, engrave the puncheons, and have the types ready for composition, with all the necessary fittings of a printing-house.

We take the date of 1469 (old style), knowing well that it should be 1470 (new style), **because it** was inscribed at the foot of the original portrait of Gering painted in the upper room of the late College of Montaigu: " Uldericus Guernich Proto-Typographus Parisiis, 1469." (See the portrait of Gering reproduced as frontispiece in Greswell's *Annals of Parisian Typography*.)

(19) " Misisti nuper ad me suavissimas Gasparini Pergamensis epistolas non a t e modo diligenter emendatas sed a tuis quoque Germanis impressoribus nitide et terse transcriptas."

(20) " Et enim quos ad hanc urbem e tua Germania librarios ascivisti quam emendatos libros ad exemplaria reddunt."

(21) " Idque tute macto studio conaris ut ne ullum quidem opus ab illis prius exprimatur quam sit a te coactis exemplaribus multis castigatum litera multa."

(22) The dialogue is anonymous in this edition, but it is positively ascribed to Heynlin (Joannes de Lapide) by Tritheim, Abbot of Spanheim, a contemporary, in his *Catalogus scriptorum ecclesiasticorum.*

(23) The fact appears from copies known without the additions. The copy in the public library at Toulouse, which is in its original oak boards, begins with two blank leaves belonging to the first printed sheet, and ends with a blank leaf belonging to the last sheet.

(24) We for the first time published the extracts of the letter of Fichet to Gaguin relative to the invention of printing by Gutenberg in *Le Livre* (1883, pp. 369-72). Four years after (in 1887) the whole text was published at Basel by Dr. Sieber, and in 1889 a photo-engraved facsimile of it was issued at Paris, with an historical notice by M. Léopold Delisle, the eminent director of the Bibliothèque Nationale.

(25) A thing to notice here is that Michael Freyburger is not named first as in the preceding volume. He resigns his place to Ulric Gering. At other times we shall find Martin Crantz named first; at others Freyburger will again be in front. We cannot conjecture any reason for these changes of order, except, perhaps, mutual deference, or the more or less labour which each partner may have bestowed on the work.

(26) In a contemporary inscription, the Sallust printed at the Sorbonne is called "Fichetanus Salustius." In consequence, we give here the name of Fichet's press to the printing establishment, presumed to be the property of the publisher

(27) " Haec autem omnia *jam diu* misimus." (See the MS. copy of the correspondence between Fichet and Cardinal Bessario [1470-71], 5th and 3rd letters, Bibliothèque Nationale, Latin MSS., 4to, No. 18,591.)

(28) The letter of Bessario is dated from Rome, the 29th of November, 1471 (*Ex Urbe, die XXVIIII novembris MCCCCLXXI*). This document begins thus : " Reverende pater, amice noster, litteras vestras accepimus quibus nobis commendas fratrem quondam Rubertum Gagginum [*sic*] quem (quia littere nostre ita nobis faciunt commendatum) libentissime vidimus eique omnem favorem nostram optulimus causa vestra, quamvis eo non indiguerit, quod ei non fuerat opus. In his autem litteris vestris quas nobis frater Rubertus (de quo in inicio diximus) reddidit . . . " (Correspondence of Fichet with Bessario, 6th letter).

(29) See Madden, *Lettres d'un Bibliographe*, 5th Series, p. 160.

(30) Copies of the Sallust are in the Spencer-Rylands Library at Manchester, and in the Bodleian at Oxford. There is also a copy in the British Museum, but it wants the *Jugurtha*.

(31) "Ce qui pourrait indiquer que G. Fichet a été le principal promoteur de l'édition" (Philippe, J., *Origine de l'Imprimerie à Paris*; Paris, 1885, p. 82).

(32) Van Praet, *Catalogue des livres imprimés sur vélin de la Bibliothèque du Roi*; Paris, 1822, 8vo, 1st part, vol. v., pp. 58, 59.

(33) Copies are to be found in the Spencer-Rylands Library and at the British Museum.

(34) "Tamen mittere statuimus Orationes quasdam hoc tempore a nobis editas pro gravissimis periculis que Italie christianisque omnibus imminent. . . . Ex Urbe, die xiiij decembris MCCCCLXX" (Correspondence between Fichet and Bessario, 3rd letter).

(35) "Posteaquam mihi tuas litteras simulque librorum fascem reddidit tuus abbas Sancti Cornelii aditus omnes militaris furor occupavit" (see printed dedicatory letter of Fichet's *Rhetoric* to Bessario, No. 1, Bibliothèque Nationale, Réserve, Z. 1683, 4to).

"Opus namque Bessarionis reverendissimi Niceni cardinalis in ipso pene medio bellorum estu mihi cum litteris fuit redditum" (see MS. dedicatory letter to Humbert Martin, Abbot of Citeaux, No. 9, National Library, Latin MSS., 4to, No. 18,591).

(36) "Ille [Bessario] superioribus mensibus lucubrationes quas christiane salutis causa per Italiam edidisset ad me diligenter in Gallias misit litteratorieque mandavit ut principibus et aliis qui Christianis prodesse, obesse Turco precibus armisve possunt earum foret legendarum opera mea potestas" (MS. dedicatory letter to the monks of the Order of Cluny, No. 16, Bibliothèque Nationale).

(37) "Studiorum meorum educator et reliquorum (si que fortassis majora succedant) excitator bonorum meorum magnificus" (manuscript dedicatory letter for the Orations, No. 1, Bibliothèque Nationale).

(38) "Que sit erga Bessarionem Nicenum cardinalem tua benevolentia prestantissime pater nequaquam sum nescius. Eas namque laudes adhuc recenti memoria teneo quibus eum tanquam sapientum seculi nostri facile principem predicabas quem Educ Lucenaique mutuos pro tua facilitate hominibus sermones miscebamus, quo fit ut opus ejus . . . non dubitem avidissime lecturum" (manuscript dedicatory letter, No. 1, for the Orations, Bibliothèque Nationale).

(39) Another manuscript copy of these letters exists, written partly on paper and partly on vellum. It is evidently copied from the former, but does not give the annotations of Fichet. It contains also the Orations of Bessario, but they are in manuscript instead of being in print. The motto, "Orta queque cadunt," is placed on the first page, and there is a note at the end, in a handwriting of the fifteenth century, "Hic liber meus est teste. *De Veteri Castro.*" This is the name of the secretary of Cardinal Rolin, the protector of Fichet, who was very likely so intimate with him as to have had leave to transcribe the letters from the copy-book of Fichet. After belonging to him, this manuscript formed part of the celebrated collection of President Bouhier of Dijon in the seventeenth century. It is now in the Bibliothèque Nationale (Latin MSS., 4to, No. 1683). The letters of Fichet and Bessario have been published by Mons. Émile Legrand in his *Cent dix Lettres Grecques de Philelphe*; Paris, Em. Leroux, 1892, 8°, pp. 223-289.

(40) In his official capacity he acted also in the schools of the Sorbonne as professor of theology. "Sive theologiam mane, sive rhetoricam post meridiem pluribus annis quotidie docendo" (see printed letter to Guillaume Chartier, Bishop of Paris, 5th letter in the collection of the dedication-letters for the *Rhetoric*, Bibliothèque Nationale, Réserve, Z. 1683, 4to).

(41) "Eodem namque die (quod dicerim citra jactanciam), non solum semel quotidie et bis etiam plerumque theologiam lectionem in refertissima auditorum corona persolvebam, sed et Rhetoricam quoque (quem nunc ad te tanquam auditorii tui fructum aliquem ipse mitto) similiter et scribebam et transcribentibus membratim proferebam, transcriptamque docebam" (MS. letter of dedication to Humbert Martin, Abbot of Citeaux, 9th letter, Bibliothèque Nationale).

"Transcribentibus" means here the workers of the new art of writing, "nova ars scribendi," viz., the printers. There are numerous examples of this expression used as synonymous with *printed* in the fifteenth century. Fichet employs it in the preface of the first book printed at the Sorbonne. "Misisti ad me suavissimas Gasparini Pergamensis epistolas . . . a tuis Germanis impressoribus nitide et terse transcriptas."

(42) A copy of the *Rhetoric*, No. 274 in the *Catalogue des Incunables des bibliothèques publiques de Lyon*, par M. Pellechet (Lyon, 1893), contains as fly-leaves duplicates of pp. 64 and 72 printed on vellum, exhibiting notable differences in the text. Another copy, which seems to be a fragment of proof, is in the University Library at Freiburg (see *Centralblatt*, v., 204).

(43) "Acceperam jam dudum Serenissime Princeps cum ab aliis tuis meritis . preclaram domi tue bibliothecam extruxisse eamque multis et exquisitissimis auctorum illustrium operibus exornasse. In quo quidem ego tuum consilium maxime laudo maximeque admiror qui non solum opes et multas compluribus seculi tui doctissimis hominibus sepe magnificeque contulisti . . . Nobilissimis principibus . . . novum iter primus omnium in Galliis reclusisti. Et enim apud ceteras nationes qui maximis laudibus celebrantur bibliothecarum structura gloriam imprimis sibi pepererunt. Ita nimium apud nos qui praeter te fuerit invenio neminem. . . . Constant Parisii bibliothecae quam plurimae, at vero qui unus unam egregiis auctoribus inferserit (te dempto) scio neminem Bibliothecae nomen gloriaque vigebit totiens de te tuaque bibliothecaria laude per urbes, flexusque maris linguae loquentur" (dedicatory letter for the *Rhetoric*, MS. letter at the end, Bibliothèque Nationale, Reserve Z, 1683, 4to).

(44) In the letter addressed to Humbert Martin, Fichet apologizes for not having written to him sooner: "Tibique fuissem pro more meo tum meis litteris gratulatus, nisi me quotidianum docendi munus plurimum impedivisset ut ne vix inter prandendum interque dormitandum aut manus a penna aut oculus a libris aut lingua parumper a docendi munere laxaretur . . . postea quam vero quam inestivus ex improbo labore morbus eversit qui meis necessarium immodestis laboribus vigiliisque modum imposuit" (MS. dedicatory letter for Bessario's *Orations*, 9th letter, Bibliothèque Nationale).

(45) A photographic facsimile of this miniature is given in Philippe's *Origine de l'Imprimerie à Paris*, p. 114.

(46) The printed letters in the volume are arranged in the following order:

1. To Cardinal Bessario. Subscribed: "Aedibus Sorbonae Parisii scriptum impressumque anno uno et septuagesimo quadringentesimoque supra millesimum." 1471. No date of month.

2. To the Pope Sixtus IV. Subscribed: "Aedibus Sorbonae Parisii scriptum pridie Kalendas septembris, anno uno et septuagesimo quadringentesimo supra millesimum." 31st of September, 1471.

3. To René, King of Sicily. Subscribed: "Parisii aedibus Sorbone, idibus quintilibus scriptum anno uno et septuagesimo quadringentesimo supra millesimum." 15th of July, 1471.

4. To John Rolin, Bishop of Autun, Cardinal of St. Stephen in Mount Coelio. Subscribed: "Aedibus Sorbonae scriptum, anno septuagesimo et quadringentesimo supra millesimum." There is an evident mistake, the word *uno* has been omitted. 15th of July, 1471.

The copies for the King of Sicily and for the bishop were ready the same day.

5. To Guillaume Chartier, Bishop of Paris. Only subscribed, "Vale." No date.

The manuscript letters are:

1. To Charles, Duke of Aquitaine, son of Charles VII., King of France. No date.

2. To Francis, Duke of Brittany. Subscribed: " Edibus Sorbone, idibus Septembris scriptum. Anno uno et septuagesimo quadragintesimo supra millesimum." 13th of September.

3. To Charles, Count of Maine. Subscribed: "In Parisiorum Sorbona. Kalendis Juliis 1471." 1st of July, 1471.

(47) The use of red in the books printed at the Sorbonne is so uncommon and exceptional that we can only trace one other example of this peculiarity. Brunet, in the *Manuel du Libraire*, ii., 1498, mentions a copy of Gasparino's letters with the heading of the text printed in red. We think that it may probably have been the cardinal's copy.

(48) See dedicatory letter of the *Rhetoric* to Guillaume Chartier (Guilielmo Quadrigario), Bishop of Paris (Bibliothèque Nationale). It comes fifth among the printed letters, and is undated.

(49) The *Orations* printed on the 23rd of April had not reached their author four months after their publication. Bessario writes on the 31st of August to his friend that he chanced to meet at Rome a secretary of the King of France, who told him that he had seen in Fichet's hands the *Orations*, which were printed and already in circulation: "Qui nobis affirmavit sese vidisse orationes in vestris manibus vestra opera impressas et traditas compluribus" (Correspondence of Bessario with Fichet, 4th letter, Bibliothèque Nationale).

(50) Laurent Bureau, born at Liernais in Burgundy, was one of the Fellows (*socii*) of the Sorbonne. He entered the Carmelite order, and preached in several places. In the year 1487 he was at Lyons. We trace his presence in this city from a note made in a copy (in our own collection) of *Ludolphi Vita Christi*, a book given to him by Jacques Buyer, the brother of Bartholomew Buyer, the first printer at Lyons. On the first (blank) leaf we read: "Hoc volumen de vita Christi gratis et ob Dei amorem mihi

fratri Laurentio Burelli theologo doctore dedit vir insignis civis Lugdunensis magister Jacobus Buerii eo anno quo Lugduni terciam quadragesimam predicavi qui fuit millesimus cccc^{mus} lxxxvij^{mus} teste signo suo manuali hic apposito.—Buyer." On the reverse of the last printed leaf, opposite the mark of J. Siber, the printer of the edition, Bureau wrote in two lines: "Anno domini Mille^{mo} lxxxvij° hic liber mihi gratis datus est.— Burelli." He was also appointed confessor of Anne, Duchess of Brittany. At the end of his life he retired to the Carmelite convent at Semur in Burgundy. The books which belonged to him are mostly editions printed by Gering. . They are scattered in the public libraries of Semur and Dijon, where we have seen them. Some are also in the Bibliothèque Nationale at Paris.

(51) See Philippe, *Origine de l'Imprimerie à Paris*, pp. 66, 67.

(52) The Bouhier MS. (Bibliothèque Nationale, Latin MSS., 4to, No. 18,591), which follows exactly Fichet's original copy-book, stops with the same catchword.

(53) According to Brunet, five copies at least of Fichet's *Rhetoric* were printed on vellum. One, the copy of Pope Sixtus IV., is in the British Museum, another is in the Imperial Library at Vienna, and a third in the Bibliothèque Nationale at Paris.

(54) A copy of the *Rhetoric* on paper is in the Spencer-Rylands Library.

(55) Our collation is taken from the copy in the public library of Toulouse, in its original oak boards. The back being rather loose, we were enabled to count exactly the number of quires.

(56) "Nuper quom apud regem . . . exitum rerum mihi creditarum opperirer, inciderunt forte in manus meas opera multa Ciceronis quae Turonem externi quidam librarii (quos dicimus impressores) advexerant."

(57) "Eorum mihi lectio fuit in hoc curiali tumultu non ingrata multoque jocundior quem quom eadem domi saepe saepiusque legebam."

(58) "Fuisset autem longe jucundior si correctissimus et capitibus distinctissimis liber quisque fuisset quemadmodum Ciceronis Orator, Valerius Maximus, et Laurentius opera tua sunt impressi."

(59) "Rogatum itaque te volo ut Ciceronis Officia (quae Parisienses librarii non longo post tempore sunt impressuri) prius isto castigandi tuoque distinguendi labore reddantur meliora."

(60) The Bibliothèque Nationale at Paris possesses a copy of the *De Officiis* printed at the Sorbonne, with a contemporary note of a former owner stating that the book was bought by him in 1471. As Easter fell this year on the 29th of March, and the letter of Fichet is dated the 7th of March, the edition was necessarily issued in the interval between the 7th and the 29th of that month, in what we call 1472(new style).

(61) The copy presented to George of Baden was in the possession of the Jesuits of Nancy in the eighteenth century. It passed afterwards into the celebrated collection of the Duc de La Vallière, and is now in the Bibliothèque Nationale. A copy on paper, of course without the letter, is in the Spencer-Rylands Library.

(62) Aug. Bernard, Madden, and Philippe are rightly of a different opinion.

(63)   Quem si cephaleis vulgaribus annotavi
                His libris veniam lector humane dabis

> Nos quoque quom legeris, pretium ne, quaeso, recuses
> Artificum ingenuae quos meruere manus.
> Pro quibus optandi mihi si nunc copia adesset
> Tam bene pro meritis commoda mille precer."

(64) A copy of the *Tusculanae Quaestiones* is in the Spencer-Rylands Library.

(65) "Ejusque legendi tanta me rapuit aviditas ut artem dormiendi per has Paschales noctes quaesitam non mihi sed ne hospiti quidem Platoni invenierim" (see Fichet's correspondence with Bessario, 10th letter, Bibliothèque Nationale).

(65*b*) "Ille me rerum venustissimarum admiratione quas nunquam legissem **tenuit** imprimis attentum."

(66) "Unum abs te peto et obtestor. Ut praefationem ad Scholam Parisiensem scribas qua mihi praecipias ut tuo nomine tuum Platonem Parisiensibus nostris exhibeamus faciamque cuique illius transcribendi facultatem" (Fichet's correspondence with Bessario, 10th letter, Bibliothèque Nationale).

(67) "Idque citissime confeceris universae namque Parisiensi scholae (quom in unum post hac Paschales ferias primum coierit) a me tuo nomine tuus Plato offeratur" (*ib.*).

(68) "Ut eo longissimo aevo publicis Collegiorum nostrorum bibliothecis apponi faciam opus tuum legatur" (*ib.*).

(69) The letter transcribed at the end of Fichet's correspondence with Bessario is dated: "Apud Sanctum Mathurinum in nostra generali congregatione (que prima fuit post Pascham) scriptum quarto nonas maias Anno secundo et septuagesimo quadringentesimo supra millesimum." It is the 14th letter.

(70) The copyists are styled "Egregii mei scriptores" by Fichet in the letter of dedication to Jehan Choard (Bibliothèque Nationale, Latin MSS., 16mo, No. 16,580).

(71) "Magni divinique Platonis epystolas meo nomine jussi tibi reddi. . . . Has si quidem ut tibi vel domi vel ruri facile in manibus essent enchyridionis instar transcribi feci" (letter of dedication, Bibliothèque Nationale, Latin MSS., 16mo, No. 16,580).

(72) A facsimile of the first page of this edition of the Letters of Plato is given in Philippe's *Origine de l'Imprimerie à Paris*, p. 147.

(73) Philippe says that some copies of the Letters of Brutus seem to have been issued separately.

(74) Chevillier, p. 52.

(75) A copy of the Letters of Phalaris, Brutus, and Crates exists in the Spencer-Rylands Library. Another (the Didot copy) is in the collection of the earliest books printed in different towns formed by Mr. Rush-Hawkins at New York.

(76) Philippe, pp. 137-139.

(77) Philippe, pp. 165-168.

(78) The piece of poetry giving in acrostic the name of Pierre Doriolle has been published by M. Léopold Delisle in the *Bibliothèque de l'Ecole des Chartes*, 1884, vol. xlv., p. 702.

(79) The word *cultori* seems here to mean more than a lover, an *admirer*, a *votary*, someone feeling a particular delight in reading the Latin poet.

(80) This manuscript of Juvenal, formerly in our possession, passed into the collections

of the late Mons. Perdrix and of Mons. Reveilhac at Evreux. It is preserved now in a private library in England.

(81) One of Fichet's servants or messengers, sent on certain business to Rome, had accepted from Bessario fifteen ducats to pay the expenses of printing the *Orations*. Fichet refused to receive the money. He writes to his friend that he had given strict orders, not once but repeatedly, to his messengers, who had to convey copies of the *Orationes* to princes and other persons, not to accept anything offered, and from Bessario least of all. He had examined the accounts, paid them all, and will not have anything to do with Bessario's ducats. If another time his servant infringes his instructions, assuredly he shall not eat his bread one day more. " Unum illud impatientissime tuli quod a te ducatos XV N. meus desumpsit. Nam ut aliis qui tuas orationes principibus ceterisque reddiderunt ne quicquam vel oblatum inde sumerent prohibui sic N quoque semel et saepius idem districtius vetueram presertim a te. . . . De sumptu, de stipendio facto rationem habui singulaque dissolvi. De tuis ducatis ne verbum quidem unum audire volui. Ex inobedientia . . . illi certe polliceor, si quid tale post hac commiserit panem meum ne die quidem uno comedet" (Correspondence of Fichet with Bessario, 10th letter, 4th of April, 1472).

(81*b*) The copy sent to Jacques d'Armagnac, Duc de Nemours, is one of these. It is exhibited in the Mazarine Gallery of the Bibliothèque Nationale, and bears the autograph signature of its former owner (see a facsimile in Thierry-Poux, *Premiers monuments de l'Imprimerie en France au XVe siècle*, Pl. iv., No. 6. The type of the dedicatory letter appears much heavier than in the text of the book itself, and shows evidently that the two impressions were not executed simultaneously, but were separated by a certain interval of time.

(82) "Omnibus autem et mihi (vel quibus ad eos deferenda tua munera commiseram) quicquam obtulerunt, una fuit responsio respuendique ratio! Quod non Fichetus sed Bessario, non ad te questum sed ad tuendam Christianitatem illis sua reddi munera librosque jussisset" (Correspondence of Fichet with Bessario, 9th letter, 21st of March, 1472, before Easter).

(83) "Vel oblatum quicquam excepi nisi duntaxat a Fratrum Minimorum ministro provinciali litteras participationis bonorum operum fratrum sororumque sue provincie quas marsupiolo quodam inclusas reverenter accepi, regumque omnium thesauris antepono" (Correspondence of Fichet with Bessario, 9th letter).

(84) "Neque de sex et quadraginta tuarum orationum opusculis quae circumquaquam per Gallias et Germanias a me fidei tuende causa sunt dispersa gratisque data" (Correspondence of Fichet with Bessario, 9th letter).

We know the names of only seventeen of those to whom they were offered. They are enumerated by Van Praet, pp. 19-23 of his *Catalogue des livres imprimés sur vélin* (2nd part, vol. ii.), from the letter-book of Fichet.

(84*b*) Madden (*Lettres d'un Bibliographe*, vol. v., p. 163) commits a gross blunder when he places the date of the presentation of the manuscript copy to Louis XI. a year before, in 1471. The 21st of March, 1471, belongs to what we call 1472. Van Praet (*Catalogue des livres imprimés sur vélin*, 2nd part, vol. ii., p. 17) had made the mistake before him.

(85) " Revertor in scholam nostram Parisiensem causa fidei (quam mihi jam dudum imposuisti) regi nobilibusque regiis exposita" (Correspondence of Fichet with Bessario, 9th letter).

(86) "Sagacissimo autem viro M. Guillelmo Ficheto prædicto qui suarum literarum communicatione nos dignatus est decorare, gratias ingentissimas referre voluit præfata natio (Picardorum); literas quoque decrevit ad gratias agendum summo nostro Pontifici pro tanto munere collato" (*Partie des pièces qui concernent l'estat présent et ancien de l'Université de Paris*; Paris, imprimé chez Jean Julien, imprimeur et libraire-juré de l'Université, 1653. 4to. 3rd series of pieces, p. 13).

Some weeks before, after his departure from the Sorbonne, Fichet had been received canon of Geneva through his brother, Mamert Fichet, Bishop "in partibus" of Hebron, "**Veneris** XVI. mensis Octobris 1472, Dominus Guillelmus Fichet fuit receptus in canonicatu, in persona domini Ebrinensis fratris ejus" (Archives cantonales de Genève, B. 3).

(86*b*) They were incorporated with the library of the College of the Sorbonne at the time of the French Revolution. When the property of the convents and religious houses was confiscated, they were sent with others to the Bibliothèque Nationale, where they are now preserved.

(87) Royer could reckon with confidence on the liberality of Cardinal Rolin, Bishop of Autun. A few years after (in 1480), the building of the old library was much damaged and decayed. The college had no money to have it rebuilt. Under these circumstances, Master Jean Royer commissioned the provisor to see the Bishop of Autun, who had formerly promised a sum of money for the expenses of the work. "Qui alias ad hoc opus perficiendum promiserat suas manus adjuvantes porrigere." A few days after, Royer reported to his companions that the bishop had promised and given to the provisor a hundred francs to begin with—"centum franchos pro inicio promisit se daturum quos postmodum juxta promissum contulit." See *Regesta Priorum*, p. 148.

In a letter of the 6th of July, 1475, the last that Gaguin wrote to Fichet, Gaguin is in great **anxiety. His** letters remained unanswered, and he had received no news from him for nearly two years. He heard only through Jean Royer that Fichet had been very ill (see Philippe, *Guillaume Fichet*, p. 158).

Jean Royer became afterwards canon of Tournai and chancellor of the church of Amiens. He died on the 20th of December, 1500. He was born at Poligny in Burgundy, and left a great number of books to the library of the College of the Sorbonne.

(88) A copy of this edition of Terence, also imperfect at the beginning, was advertised in the 282nd catalogue of J. Baer, at Frankfort (1892), No. 1083.

BIBLIOGRAPHY.

BIBLIOGRAPHY.

I. GASPARINI EPISTOLAE.   N. D.   4º.

  COLLATION: [a-l¹⁰, m⁸] no printed signatures[1] or catchwords; 118 ff., 22 ll.

  REGISTER: *a* 2ª, GVILLERMVS; *b* 1ª, potest; *c*, rebus; *d* [C]Vm modestiam; *e*, atq̃ sociis; *f*, sit in; *g*, ne id; *h*, studia; *i*, uel consulendo; *k*, nulla; *l*, me iactura; *m*, habui.

  DESCRIPTION: Fo. 1 blank; Fo. 2ª, GVILLERMVS Fichetus **parifienfis** ∥ theologus doctor / Ioanni Lapidano Sor- ∥ bonensis scholæ priori salutem; Fo. 2ᵇ, line 19, Vale. & me dilige/ te amantē. Scriptum ∥ apud sorbonā ! uelocissima fichetea manu ; ∥ Fo. 3ª, line 1, Gasparini pergamensis clariffimi orato- ∥ ris / epistolaꝗ liber foeliciter incipit; ∥ *End*. Fo. 118ª, line 11, Foelix Epl'aꝗ Gasparini finis ; [line 12 blank].

  Vt Sol lumen !   sic doctrinam fundis in orbem
  Musarum nutrix / regia parisius ;
  Hinc prope diuinam / tu quā germania nouit
  Artem scribendi ! suscipe promerita ;
  Primos ecce libros ! quos hæc industria finxit
  Francorum in terris. ædibus atq̃ tuis ;
  Michael Vdalricus / Martinusq̃ magistri
  Hos impresserunt. ac facient alios ;

Fo. 118ᵇ blank.

  WATERMARKS: Anchor; large fleur-de-lis crowned, with the letter J at end.

  REMARKS: In all copies the first three letters of the name Vdalricus in the metrical colophon are written by hand, in imitation of the type, to

---

[1] Most of the Sorbonne books have MS. signatures written in a single hand. They are placed, as usual, at the extreme edge, where the binder's knife has often injured or destroyed them.

correct some such misprint as *Et Vlricus* or *Et Vdalricus*. Similar MS. corrections are to be found on fol. 2 (first page of text), l. 9, where *debeat*, and fol. 51, l. 16, where *ullum*, is added in the margin, with the usual typographic sign of intercalation. In the last line of fol. 4ᵇ the omitted word *tpibus* is added by hand, and on fol. 34ᵃ *et* is corrected into *est*.

COPIES KNOWN: British Museum; John Rylands Library, Manchester; Bibliothèque Nationale, Paris, 2 copies; Bibliothèque de Besançon; Library of the late Duc d'Aumale, Chantilly; Royal Library, the Hague; Biblioteca Palatina, Parma; Imperial Library, Vienna.

II. GASPARINI ORTHOGRAPHIA. N. D. 4°.

COLLATION: [a-h¹⁰; i-k¹²; l-x¹⁰; y-z⁸; aa²] no printed signatures or catchwords; 232 ff., 23 ll.

REGISTER: a^2, GASPARINI; b, perueniet; c, quod; d, illos; e, Et; f, nimis; g, in; h, Arra; i, nymphe; k, as; l, præpositio; m, Ferrugo; n, Hemis; o, In; p, Vide; q, Milonis; r, Oculatus; s, Phœnissa; t, adiciuntur; u, Secius; x, Symposium; y, sit; z, Est diphtongandi; aa, dum pronuntias!

DESCRIPTION: Fo. 1 and 2 blank; Fo. 3ᵃ, GASPARINI Pergamensis/ Or- ‖ thographiæ liber foeliciter incipit; Fo. 219ᵃ, line 8, Orthographiæ Gasparini Secun- ‖ da pars foeliciter finit; Fo. 219ᵇ, 220 blank; Fo. 221ᵃ, Est diphtongandi ratio (sic credo) sepulta ‖ Gasparine tua. Viue Guarine doce; ‖ Guarini Veronensis / de diphtongis ‖ libellus foeliciter incipit; Fo. 221ᵇ, Compendiosus de arte punctandi ‖ dialogus foeliciter incipit; *End*. Fo. 231ᵃ, line 9, FINIS; Fo. 231ᵇ, 232, blank.

WATERMARKS: The crowned fleur-de-lis with letter J at the end; a P gothic with a small cross at the top; an unicorn.

REMARKS: One copy is at present known with six additional printed leaves (the last being blank), not included in our collation. It contains the text of a letter addressed by Fichet to Robert Gaguin,.in which the right of Gutenberg to the invention of printing is formally attested by the printers of the Sorbonne. This letter is subscribed Fo. 4ᵇ, line 16, Aedibus sorbonç raptim a me kalēdis Ianua ‖ riis diluculo scriptum; without date of the year, and is followed on Fo. 5 by a poetical piece, by Robert Gaguin, in praise of his friend Fichet, written on the following day. These most interesting documents were published by the late Dr. Sieber at Basel in 1887, and entirely reproduced in facsimile, with an introduction by Mons. Léopold Delisle, at Paris in 1889. Copies of the *Orthographia* are to be found without the "Diphtongandi ratio" by Guarinus and the dialogue "de arte punctandi" composed by Heynlin.

COPIES KNOWN: Bibliothèque Nationale, Paris; Bibliothèque Mazarine, Paris; Bibliothèque de Toulouse, copy without the tracts of Guarinus and Heynlin; University Library, Basel, copy with the letter of Fichet; University Library, Freiburg im Breisgau, the letter of Fichet only (see below, p. 56).

III. SALLUSTIUS. N. D. 4°.

COLLATION: [a-b¹⁰, c-d⁸, e-f¹⁰; g-i⁸; k-l¹²; m⁴] no printed signatures or catchwords. 106 ff., 23 ll.

REGISTER: *a* 1ᵃ, Caii Crispi; *b*, magna merces; *c*, tandū !; *d*, eam/; *e*, Caii Crispi; *f*, curia egrediūt; *g*, nisi demū; *h*, frequentes; *i*, bat ubi; *k*, iusq̨ modi; *l*, ex cohortibus; *m*, est quo.

DESCRIPTION: Fo. 1ᵃ, Caii Crispi Salustii / de Lucii ‖ Catilinæ coniuratione liber ‖ foeliciter incipit; Fo. 35ᵃ, line 9, C. Crispi Salustii de coniuratione ‖ Catilinæ liber / foeliciter finit; Fo. 35ᵇ blank; Fo. 36 blank; Fo. 37ᵃ, Caii Crispi Salustii / de bello Iu- ‖ gurthæ contra populum Romanum ‖ liber / foeliciter incipit; *End.* Fo. 105ᵃ, line 11, C. Crispi Salustii de bello Iugur- ‖ thino liber foeliciter finit;

     De morte Iugurthę disticon;
   Qui cupis ignotum / Iugurthæ noscere letum !
   Tarpeiæ rupis / trusus ad ima ruit ;
     [Line 16 blank.]
   Nunc parat arma uirosq̨, sil rex maximus orbis !
    Hostibus antiquis exitum minitans.
   Nunc igitur bello studeas gens pariseorum !
    Cui martis quondam gloria magna fuit.
   Exemplo tibi sint nunc fortia **facta uirorum !**
    Quæ digne memorat Crispus in hoc opere.
   Armigerisq̨, tuis alemannos adnumeres ! qui
    Hos pressere libros arma futura tibi ;

Fol. 105ᵇ, 106 blank.

WATERMARKS: Large fleur-de-lis crowned, with the letter J at end.

REMARKS: The first lines of the copy on vellum preserved in the Bibliothèque Nationale differ from those of the copies on paper: Caii Crispi Salustii / nobilissimi ciuis ‖ ac consularis romani / de Lucii Catilinæ ‖ coniuratione liber / foeliciter incipit; in the same copy there is a MS. correction, *ium* ‖ *ma* / at **the** end of line 2 and beginning of line 3 in the text. At the foot of the page the words *Fichetanus Salustius* **are** written in a contemporary hand.

COPIES KNOWN: British Museum [without the *Jugurtha*]; Bodleian Library, Oxford; John Rylands Library, Manchester; Bibliothèque Nationale, Paris, 2 copies, one on paper and another on vellum; Bibliothèque de l'Arsenal, Paris; Bibliothèque de Reims; Bibliothèque d'Angers; Bibliothèque de Bourges; Bibliothèque de St. Brieuc; University Library, Basel (Heynlin's copy); Imperial Library, Vienna; University Library, Freiburg.

IV. Florus. N. D. 4º.

COLLATION: [a-f¹⁰, g⁸, h-i¹⁰, k⁴] no printed signatures or catchwords; 90 ff., 23 ll.

REGISTER: a 1ᵇ, In. L. Annei; b, urbium stragem; c, consulum interceptus; d, darium cogitarent; e, pitudini; f, hac mirer; g, & ingenuis; h, Incipit liber quartus; i, ros! aut cæsar; k, intentum.

DESCRIPTION: Fo. 1ᵃ blank; Fo. 1ᵇ, In. L. Annei Flori Epithoma de hystoria || Titi Liuii / Argumentū foeliciter ¡incipit; End. Fo. 89ᵃ, line 5, L. Annei Flori Epitoma de || Tito Liuio / finit liber quartus;
[Line 8 blank.]

    Robertus Gaguinus / Lucei Annei
    Flori lectoribus / salutem optat;
  Quos nulla in terris concluserat ora quirites
  Hæc flori obstrictos parua tabella capit.
  Et quæque / eximia produxit Liuius arte /
  Bella / duces / pompas / rite coacta tenet.
  Quo uere exemplo / uobis sperate futuṣ /
  Qui fama / & quæstu / fertis in astra gradum.
  Post tumidos nisus / post sæua pericula sortis
  Ad manes raptos / uos breuis urna teget;
      Valete;

Fo. 89ᵇ, 90, blank.

WATERMARK: The fleur-de-lis with letter J at end.

REMARKS: By a pen correction on the 6th verse of Robert Gaguin's final address to the reader, the word printed *fertur* is altered to *fertis*.

COPIES KNOWN: British Museum; John Rylands Library, Manchester; Bibliothèque Nationale, Paris; Bibliothèque Mazarine, Paris [wants fol. 1, containing the *Argumentum*]; Bibliothèque de Reims, 3 copies; Bibliothèque d'Angers (bound with Phalaris and Plato); Bibliothèque de St. Brieuc; University Library, Basel (Heynlin's copy bound with the *Sallust*); Biblioteca Mediceo-Laurenziana, Florence.

V. Bessarionis Orationes. 1471. 4º.

COLLATION: [a-d¹⁰] no printed signatures or catchwords; 40 ff., 23 ll., except fo. 30ᵃ, which has 22 ll. only; fo. 30ᵇ, 24 ll.; fo. 32ᵇ, 24 ll.

REGISTER: a 1ᵃ, Reuerendo; b, runt! si; c, orta!; d, decernenda.

DESCRIPTION: Fo. 1ᵃ, Reuerendo & doctissimo patri magistro || Guilielmo ficheti sacræ theologię pfes- || sori in collegio Sorbonæ Parisii amico || nostro carissimo! Bessario episcopus sabi- || nensis cardinalis / patriarcha constantino- || politanus nicenus; Fo. 29ᵇ, EIVSDEM ad eosdem persuasio! || ex auctoritate Demosthenis; Fo. 30ᵇ, DEMOSTHENIS ORATIO || pro ferenda ope olynthiis aduersus Philippū || regem Macedonnm (*sic*); End. Fo. 39ᵃ, line

16, ut omni ad id studio incumbatis quantis ma- | ximis possum precibus oro / atq, obtestor ; ‖ FINIS ; Fo. 39ᵇ, 40 blank.

WATERMARK : The anchor, with a cross in the middle at the end.

REMARKS : Copies were sent to kings, emperors, and other potentates, as also to chiefs of monastic orders, containing dedicatory letters printed or manuscript. As they differ in each copy according to their length, we have not, of course, included them in our collation. Fo. 22ᵇ, lines 15 and 16, the space left in blank for four Greek words not printed is filled up in MS. Fo. 1ᵃ, line 4, the name of Bessario, printed wrongly *Bassario*, is corrected to *Bessario*. In Fichet's own copy the headlines 5 and 6 are partly erased and corrected with a pen, giving this reading, *cardiāl' nicen⁹ priarcha constantino- ‖ politanus* ; Fo. 10ᵇ, line 18, the word *italiam*, omitted, is added in the margin ; Fo. 17ᵃ, line 6, the words *hostis impellite*, repeated in error, are erased, blotted, or cancelled by dots in the various copies ; Fo. 17ᵇ, line 22, the word *cēsemus*, omitted, is added in MS. ; Fo. 25, line 14, the word *repugnamus* is altered to *reprimamus*.

COPIES KNOWN : John Rylands Library, Manchester ; Bibliothèque Nationale, Paris, 4 copies [1°. copy sent to Jacques d'Armagnac, Duke de Nemours, with a printed letter addressed to the king, Louis XI., the princes, dukes, and other high personages of his government ; 2°. Fichet's own copy, with his autograph corrections, preceded by the MS. copies of all the dedicatory letters ; 3°. copy sent to the abbot and monks of Cluny, with the MS. letter addressed to them ; 4°. copy sent to John Nomagian, chief of the Carthusian order, with the MS. letter addressed to him] ; Bibliothèque Mazarine, Paris [copy without corrections, but with the Greek MS. quotations on fol. 22] ; Bibliothèque de Reims, 2 copies ; Vatican Library, Rome, copy on vellum sent to Edward IV., King of England, with a printed letter of dedication and a fine miniature painting ; Imperial Library, Vienna, copy of the Emperor Frederick III., with the letter of dedication, consisting of two leaves, printed on vellum, the text of the *Orations* being on paper ; Royal Library, Turin, copy on vellum sent to Amadeus IX., Duke of Savoy, with a special printed letter. Philippe (*Origine de l'Imprimerie à Paris*, p. 100) describes this copy, and says that the book is preserved in the Royal Library at Turin ; but from a recent communication of Senator Carutti, librarian to His Majesty the King of Italy, we learn that the book is no longer in the Royal Library, nor is it in the Biblioteca Nazionale at Turin. No one knows what has become of it. Cantonal Library, Luzern [bound with the letters of Phalaris, Brutus and Crates], Erhard Windsberg's copy given by Fichet.

VI. FICHETI RHETORICA. 1471. 4°.

COLLATION : [a⁴, b-e², f-h¹⁰, i⁸, k²⁰, l⁸, m¹², n-o⁸, p¹⁰, q⁶, r¹⁰, s⁶, t¹², u⁶, x¹²] no printed signatures or catchwords ; 194 ff., 23 ll., and sometimes 24 ll.

REGISTER: *a* 1ᵃ, GVILLERMI; *b*, De quinq̢; *c*, & sententiaʀ; *d*, cilium; *c*, ʀi oporteret; *d*, uel negocia (in first printed copies, simplicem futuroʀ); *e*, mihi faciet; *f*, (P)ROPRIVM; *g*, Guillermi; *h*, perindeac (*sic*); *i*, (C)ONTRARIA; *k*, (N)OSTRAE; *l*, affectu; *m*, linguas/; *n*, Guillermi; *o*, (quasi; *p*, quidem; *q*, dicimus; *r*, uiribus; *s*, apud Terentiū!; *t*, propria!; *u*, aridam/; *x*, Ad tertii.

DESCRIPTION: Fo. 1ᵃ, GVILLERMI Ficheti Alnetani/ artium ‖ & theologiæ parisiensis doctoris/ rhetori- ‖ corum libroʀ, præfatio; Fo. 4ᵇ, line 22, Ficheteæ rhetoricæ præfatio finit. ‖ Incipit liber primus; Fo. 5ᵃ, De quinq̢, rhetoricis elemētis artem extrin- ‖ secus comprehendentibus omnem; Fo. 118, blank. *End*. Fo. 191ᵃ, line 17, In Parisioʀ, Sorbona conditæ Ficheteæ ‖ rhetoricæ finis Roberti Gaguini se- ‖ quitur panagericus (*sic*) in auctorem; Fo. 191ᵇ, Patri ac præceptori suo / Guillermo ‖ Ficheto parisiensi theologo doctori/ ‖ Robertus Gaguinus. S. P. D. [Line 4 blank.]

   (Q)Vos luteos homīes finxit natura/ deauras
   Et facis æloquio/ clare fichete deos.
   Te digna extulerit præclara lutetia cælo!
   Cui tua rectiloquos/ lingua diserta parit.
   Quæ fuit obscura! sterili ruditate loquendi!
   Fulgida nunc radiis/ arte polita micat.
   Puluerulenta situ/ & squalore uolumīa longo!
   Exiliunt tenebris en reuoluta suis.
   Per cathedras cicero uerbi pater intonat acer!
   Et ueterum mille nomina lecta uirum.
   Quos eqdē (si sensa/ aīos/ retinere putandū ē)
   Gratari inter se nunc tibi (crede) iuuat!
   Magnū aūt ē fama/ & cælum! & pulchʀ, memorarier
   Quæ probȝ et celū! quisq̢ leuet humɔ actis?
   Qui ueniet posthac/ puro sȝmone latinus;
   Inq̢ sacros aditus (quod semper græcia fecit)
   Dicendi appinget philosophia decus.

Fo. 192ᵃ. Theologi exurgent! quos tot docuisse ρbatis!
   Qui se hyeronymis assimulasse uelint;
   Ergo eris in nr̃is/ qᵉ achiuis ille ρmetheus!
   Qui terræ obstrictos igniit arte uiros.
   Siue opifex hominū/ qui duris cotibus auras!
   Indidit, illa iubens uiuere deucalion;
   Fœlix illa quidem tali sabaudia alumno!
   Cuius erit gallis perpetuatus honor;
   Gaude igit̃ doctor/ habiturus nomē in æuum!
   Gaguinumq̢ magis usq̢ benignus ama;
     Vale. Fœlixq̢ uiue;

Fo. 192ᵇ, 193, 194, blank.

WATERMARKS: A bell; a pot or jug; the anchor.

REMARKS: The dedicatory epistles, all of the year 1471, which are added to special copies, and are of different lengths, as in the *Orations* of Bessario, are not included in our collation. The first leaf of the quire *d* [Fo. 37] presents a different text in the copies printed on vellum and in some copies on paper, apparently the first issued from the press. Fo. 64 and 72 have also been reprinted with differences, as appears from cancelled leaves pasted on the inside cover of one copy. Of all the books produced by the first Parisian press, Fichet's *Rhetoric* is the one where the most numerous pen corrections or additions are to be observed. The copy presented to Charles de Bourbon, Archbishop of Lyons, now in the Bibliothèque Nationale, seems to be the most carefully revised. The corrections and alterations in this are similar to those in the copy in the Bibliothèque Mazarine at Paris. The following are the corrections in the first hundred pages: Fo. 10ᵃ, line 21, added with a pen, *orationis*; line 22, *qualitatis*; Fo. 11ᵃ, line 14, *p. se*; Fo. 14ᵃ, line 20, *priorem*; Fo. 31ᵃ, line 22, *defendi cohiberiq*; Fo. 35ᵇ, line 18, correction, *uolasse*; Fo. 38ᵃ, line 9, *præcipue*; line 16, *præcipue* again; Fo. 40ᵃ, *ueniemus*; Fo. 45ᵃ, line 6, added with a pen, *a*, and on the following line correction, *duobus consulibus*; line 13, with a pen, EQVALE *est*; line 14, correction, *paribus*; line 17, correction, *subuertit*; Fo. 46ᵃ, correction, *forem*; Fo. 47ᵃ, line 1, DIFFIGVRATIO; line 5, corrections, *cum* and *cetera*; line 12, pen correction, *societates*; line 15, *societates* again; Fo. 47ᵇ, lines 15-16, pen correction, *fortitu- | dinem*; Fo. 49ᵇ, line 9, *hermacreouti*; line 21, *odire* changed to *odisse*; Fo. 66ᵃ, line 20, *Sex*; Fo. 66ᵇ, line 4, *Tum*; line 12, *imprie*; Fo. 74ᵃ, line 2, added by hand, *i totū*; line 20, after the word *oportet* printed, the following pen addition, *nisi diuisio uel expositio locū eius obtineat*; Fo. 76ᵃ, line 18, *euidentia*; Fo. 76ᵇ, line 10, (E)VIDENTIA; line 21, correction, *iis*; Fo. 79ᵇ, line 3, MS. addition in the margin, with a sign of reference, *iterū uel alio modo narrare. Aut auditoribus ita tenet? negotiu3,/ ut nostra nihil il̃sit*; line 10, *euidentia*; line 15, *tubus*; line 23, added with a sign of reference, *et hoc*; Fo. 80ᵇ, line 11, MS. addition, *ne iterdū gdī nō excedat*; Fo. 84ᵇ, line 8, *rhetoti*, wrongly printed, is corrected to *rhetori*; line 17, added with a pen, *opposita*; Fo. 85ᵇ, line 13, added, *quadā*; Fo. 86ᵃ, line 18, correction, *solutiones*; **Fo. 86ᵇ**, line 7, correction, *inuicē sfirmāt*; Fo. 88ᵇ, line 23, pen addition, *iit*; Fo. 92ᵃ, line 15, a word partly erased and altered to VICISSITVDO; Fo. 100ᵃ, line 13, *colligatioē* corrected, and *ordiē* added. The copy on vellum at the Bibliothèque Nationale contains other MS. additions, but they seemed to us to be rather the act of a reader than of the editor of the book. For this reason we have not noticed them.

COPIES KNOWN: British Museum, Presentation copy to Pope Sixtus IV., on vellum, with a special printed letter of dedication, decorated with a fine miniature, giving the portrait of Fichet, and reproduced as a frontispiece to this monograph; John Rylands Library, Manchester; Bibliothèque Nationale,

Paris, 3 copies, 1°. A copy printed on vellum, 2°. the copy presented to Charles de Bourbon, Archbishop of Lyons, preceded by a special letter and a reprint of the dedicatory letter to Cardinal Bessarion, two additional printed leaves, with a miniature border bearing the arms of Bourbon, 3°. copy with the arms and device of Laurent Bureau, doctor of the Sorbonne; the letters to Charles de Bourbon and Cardinal Bessarion, MSS. on vellum, are added to the copy on paper, but the handwriting is a modern forgery in the old style. See above, page 15; Bibliothèque Mazarine, Paris, copy that seems to have belonged to Gabriel Naudé, librarian of Cardinal Mazarin, with a note in his handwriting; Bibliothèque de Lyon, a copy with cancelled leaves, presenting notable differences in the text, fastened to the inside of the cover; Bibliothèque d'Aix-en-Provence; St. Mark's Library, Venice, dedication copy to Cardinal Bessarion on vellum, with a special printed letter, dated 1471, decorated with a fine miniature painting and capitals illuminated in gold and colours; Imperial Library, Vienna, copy on vellum; University Library, Basel, Heynlin's copy; University Library, Breslau. A manuscript copy on vellum of the *Rhetoric*, richly illuminated, with a miniature representing the author offering his book to Charles, Count du Maine, prince of the blood royal of France, is in the ducal library at Gotha. In the University Library, Freiburg im Breisgau, are four leaves of proofs of the end of the work, exhibiting, according to Dr. F. Pfaff, a different and much shorter recension of the text, as from *Gestus* to the end there are only 20 instead of 48 articles. See the *Centralblatt für Bibliothekswesen*, vol. 5, pp. 201-206. Together with this fragment are bound four printed dedicatory letters of Fichet, viz., 1°. for Bessario's *Orations* to the Emperor Frederick; 2°. for the *Rhetoric* to Janus, Count of Genevois in Savoy (not in the collection of dedicatory letters for the *Rhetoric* at the Bibliothèque Nationale), dated 10th before the Calends of October (September 22), 1471; 3°. for the *Rhetoric* to René, King of Sicily; 4°. the letter to Robert Gaguin for his copy of the *Orthographia*, in which mention is made of Gutenberg (*Bonemontanus*); see p. 50.

VII. AUGUSTINUS DATUS. Eloquentiæ præcepta. N.D. 4°.

COLLATION: [a-d¹⁰, e⁶] no printed signatures or catchwords, 46 ff., 23 ll.
REGISTER: *a* 1ª, AVGVSTINI; *b*, eādem; *c*, bus. istis; *d*, propter; *e*, Conor.
DESCRIPTION: Fo. 1ª, AVGVSTINI DATI Senensis Isago- ‖ gicus libellus in eloquẽtiæ p̃cepta, ad An- ‖ dreã dñi christoferi filiũ fœliciter incipit; *End.* Fo. 44ᵇ, line 17, Augustini dati Senensis oratoris primarii ‖ Isagogicus libellus in elocutionis precepta finit fœliciter; Fo. 45, 46, blank.
WATERMARK: Anchor.
COPIES KNOWN: University Library, Basel, Heynlin's copy.

VIII. CICERO. DE ORATORE.
     No copy known.

IX. VALERIUS MAXIMUS.
     No copy known.

X. VALLÆ ELEGANTIÆ. 1471. Fol.

COLLATION: [a-g^{10}; h^8; i-o^{10}; p^{12}; q-z^{10}; aa-bb^{10}; cc-ee^8; ff^{10}] no printed signatures or catchwords; 284 ff., 32 ll., and sometimes only 30 ll.

REGISTER: a^1, Quot Vniuersi; b, .P. Paulus Senilis; c, e contrario; d, Seruius; e, sermonis; f, Solius; g, audientem; h, Quid; i, Incipit; k, duodeq̃dragenū; l, copias; m, (O)Ratores; n, ciantur; o, fœminū; p, possint; q, Incipit; r, gationē; s, (V)Etere; t, mori!; u, a uinea; x, qua; y, ordeacea; z, Ca. vi; aa, Laurentii; bb, mineruæ; cc, familiarissimus; dd, (S)Ecretum; ee, Elegantium; ff, Malleolus!

DESCRIPTION: Fo. 1^a, Quot Vniuersi Operis Elegantiaʀ Lau- ‖ rentii Vallæ sunt libri! quæue unicuiq̃ li- ‖ bro subiecta materia! & quis in singulis materiis pertractandis ordo seruetur; ‖ (V)NIVERSVM hoc Elegantiarum ‖ Opus/ Sex Libris Distinctum Est; Fo. 9^b, blank; Fo. 10, blank; Fo. 11^a, .P. Paulus Senilis Ioanni Heynlin de Lapide ‖ salutem plurimam dicit; Fo. 79^a, Incipit prohemium in libʀ tertium! de laude iurisconsultoʀ in Elegantia scribendi! sintque nemo/ nec in iu ‖ re! nec in logica! philosophiaq̃, proficere potest; Fo. 151^a, Incipit Prohemiū in librum quintum! Cur non ‖ plures de hac re libros condidit; Fo. 230, blank; Fo. 231, Ca. vi. ostendens causam cur suus & sui abutimur; Fo. 239^b, blank; Fo. 240, blank; Fo. 241, Laurentii Vallæ liber/ in errores Antonii Raudensis fœliciter incipit; Fo. 275, Elegantium uocabuloʀ quæ in hoc opere sparsim tradita ‖ sunt! sub principalium litterarum suarum ordine/ cum lib- ‖ roʀ capitulorumq̃ annotatione! compendiosa collectio; Fo. 282^a, Petro Paulo Senili/ christianissimi francoʀ regis secretario! Ioannes de Lapide S. P. D.; End. Fo. 282^b, two last lines, ... Aedibus sorbonę scriptū anno ‖ uno & septuagesimo quadringentesimoq̃ supra millesimum; Fo. 283 and 284, blank.

WATERMARKS: A pot or jug, with a small cross at the top; a bell; a stag's head with antlers.

REMARKS: In some copies the first quire, consisting of the table of contents and the letter of Paulus Senilis, is placed at the end, after the letter of Ioannes de Lapide, written from the Sorbonne, and dated 1471, which is a reply to that of Senilis.

COPIES KNOWN: Bodleian Library, Oxford; Bibliothèque Nationale, Paris, 2 copies (one imperfect); Bibliothèque de Toulouse; Bibliothèque de Poitiers (imperfect); Imperial Library, Vienna; University Library, Breslau.

XI. CICERO DE OFFICIIS; DE AMICITIA; DE SENECTUTE; SOMNIUM SCIPIONIS; PARADOXA. March, 1472. Fol.

COLLATION: [a⁸; b-l¹⁰; m-n⁴; o⁶; p⁸] no printed signatures or catchwords; 126 ff., 31 ll.

REGISTER: a^1, Guillermus fichætus; b, .M. Tullii; c, que spectat; d, inferior; e, quoꝗ; f, Atqᷓ huic; g, De generali; h, De quęstionibus; i, suetudo; k, q̃ cū eo; l, denī & alia!; m, (H)Ec me; n, usurpas!; o, Liber; p, .M. Tullii.

DESCRIPTION: Fo. 1ª, Guillermus fichætus parisiensis theologus doctor / ‖ Ioanni lapidano theologo p̄fessori. s. p. d.; Fo. 2ª, line 21 [end of the line], Apd ‖ Turonē ędibus hospitis mei Radulfi toustani ciuis longe hu ‖ manissimi / Anno uno & septuagesimo q̃dringentesimoꝗ, su- ‖ pra Millesimū, Nonis Martii citissime scriptum; ‖ [line 25 blank;] line 26, Ioanni Lapidano / Tetrastichon fichæteum. [Line 27 blank.]
Line 28:

  Vt puncti / cęsi / pateant libri Ciceronis!
  Guillermi suasu / sis Lapidane uigil
  Sic facili cursu / cum fruger / tum decus esse
  Tu poteris semper! clara Fichetea spes;

Fo. 2ᵇ, Io. de Lapide sacris in litteris Parisii licentiatus / ‖ .G. fichęto parisiensi theologo doctori, s. p. d.; Fo. 3ª, line 23 [end of line], Vale. Ae ‖ dibus Sorbone Parisii scriptum. [Line 25 blank;] line 26, Io. Lapidani Tetrastichon ad Guillermū fichętū. [Line 27 blank.]
Line 28:

  Accipe distinctos Guillerme libros Ciceronis.
  Si lęsi pateant! criminis auctor eris.
  Sin fuerint frugi! maior tibi q̃ Lapidano /
  Gratia debetur! laus quoqᷓ maior erit;

Fo. 3ᵇ, Vniuersi operis officioꝗ, .M. Tullii Ciceronis / cū sub- ‖ iectaꝗ, materiaꝗ, recollectione summaria partitio; Fo. 7ª, line 10 [end of line], FINIS. [line 11 blank;] line 12, Io. de Lapide / cunctis uirtutū amatoribus. s. p. d. [Line 13 blank.]
Line 14:

  Accipe consiliū quo fias officiosus,
   Et cito! si credas! hos lege sæpe libros.
  Nam docet hic Cicero quo fonte oriaī honestas!
   Effluit & uirtus omnis! & officium.
  Vtile definit & quodcunqᷓ nocluū,
   Ex hominū studiis ducere principium.
  Qualiter & possis homines tibi conciliare!
   Vt multū prosint / ac noceant minime.

Sunt qui secernant ab honestis utilitatem !
 Horũ errore nihil fedius esse probat.
Concludens nil utile / quod non semper honestũ !
 Nec sit honestũ aliquod utilitate carens.
In primis igĩ rectum statuas tibi finem !
 Turpia nec speres finibus apta tuis.
Sic uirtutis iter tutis transibis (honesti
 Officio fretus) gressibus ad superos ;

[Fo. 7ᵇ, blank ; Fo. 8 entirely blank.]

Fo. 9ᵃ, .M. Tullii Ciceronis / Arpinatis / consulis Romani / ‖ oratorumq̃, principis / ad .M. Tulliũ Ciceronẽ filiũ ‖ suum / Officioʀ, liber primus / in quo de honesto disse ‖ rĩt / foeliciter incipit ; Fo. 74ᵃ, line 26, .M. Tullii Ciceronis / officioʀ, Liber Tertius & ‖ Vltimus / in quo de comparatiõe utilis & honesti ‖ explicatum est ! fœliciter Finit ; Fo. 74ᵇ, blank ; Fo. 75ᵃ, M. T. Ciceronis liber de amicitia / tractatibus tripartĩt ; Fo. 76ᵃ, M. Tullii Ciceronis Liber de Amicitia / ad Atticum ! ‖ fœliciter incipit ; Fo. 93ᵃ, line 29, Marci Tullii Ciceronis de Amicitia Liber / ‖ ad Atticum ! foeliciter finit ; Fo. 93ᵇ, blank ; Fo. 94ᵃ, M. T. Ciceronis Liber de senectute tribus distinctus est ‖ tractatibus ; Fo. 95ᵃ, M. Tullii Ciceronis Liber de Senectute de Atticum ‖ foeliciter incipit ; Fo. 110ᵇ, line 5, M. T. ! Ciceronis de senectute ‖ ad Atticum fœliciter finit ; Fo. 111 and 112 entirely blank ; Fo. 113ᵃ, Liber de somnio Scipionis / vii capitulis distinctus est ! Fo. 114ᵃ, .M. T. Ciceronis. de Republica liber sextus q de somnio ‖ Scipionis inscribiĩ ! in **quo docet** animas bene de R. P. me- ‖ ritorum / post corpora cælo reddi & illic frui beatitudinis ‖ ppetuitate ! fœliciter incipit ; Fo. 118ᵇ, line 10, .M. T. **Ciceronis de somnio** Sci- ‖ pionis Liber fœliciter finit; Fo. 119ᵃ, .M. T. Ciceronis paradoxa incipiũt fœliciter ; End. Fo. 126ᵃ, line **31**, .M. Tullii Ciceronis paradoxa foeliciter finiunt ; Fo. 126ᵇ blank.

WATERMARK : Anchor.

REMARKS : In the first copies printed, line 23 in the text of Fichet's letter has a misprint *officiosimo*. In other copies this has been corrected to *officiosissime*, and another word, *nihil*, ending the line, is divided, *ni-* on the same line and *hil* on the beginning of the following (see Philippe, pp. 192-193). In some copies the following pen corrections are to be found. Fo. 36ᵃ, line 20, *preditus* is added ; line 21, *aptum* ; Fo. 37ᵃ, line 28, *molestias*. A copy presented by the editor Heynlin alias de la Pierre (Lapidanus) to George of Baden, Bishop of Metz, contains at the beginning an additional leaf printed on vellum, decorated with a fine illuminated initial letter. This copy is without printed titles or summaries to the chapters. They are written in red by the rubricator. Another copy presents an interesting peculiarity. A contemporary note at the end of the *Paradoxa* written on the margin states that the book (already printed, but without the *Somnium Scipionis*) was bought in Paris in 1471 (end of March, 1472).

COPIES KNOWN : British Museum ; Bibliothèque Nationale, Paris, 3 copies, the first with a printed letter of dedication on vellum, addressed to George of Baden, Bishop of Metz ; the second, without the *Somnium Scipionis*, contains the mention of having been bought in Paris at the end of March, 1472 ; the third is bound with the *Tusculanæ Quæstiones*, published by Erhard Windsberg ; Bibliothèque de Bourges ; Bibliothèque de **Toulouse**, Count Hoym's copy, bound with the *Tusculanæ Quæstiones*; University Library, Basel, bound after the *Tusculanæ Quæstiones*; Royal Library, The Hague ; Royal **Library**, Stuttgart ; Kgl. Sächsische Bibliographische Sammlung, Leipzig.

XII. CICERONIS TUSCULANÆ QUÆSTIONES. N. D. Fol.

COLLATION: [a–h¹⁰ ; i⁸] no printed signatures or catchwords, 88 ff., 31 ll.

REGISTER: *a* 1ª, M. T. C. oratoR ; *b*, haberemus ; *c*, qbus orbati ; *d*, & regina ; *e*, Cirenaicis ; *f*, admiratione ; *g*, potest ; *h*, non potest ; *i*, hesterna.

DESCRIPTION: Fo. 1ª, M. T. C. oratoR, Homeri prologus in Tusculanarum ‖ quæstionum (in quibus de maximis quæstionibus co- ‖ piose / ornateq̧ dicit) librum p̃mum fœliciter incipit ; Fo. 85ª, line 30, .M. T. Ciceronis TusculanaR, quæstionũ Liber ‖ quintus & ultimus finem habet fœlicem ; **Fo. 86ᵇ**, Erhardus Ciceronianæ lectionis amatoribus. S. P. D.

> Quom tua vel mutis tribuat eloquia uocem !
>   Quom tibi phœbeus carmina dictet honos !
> Nonne reus musis / & uatibus vsq̧ tenebor !
>   Si tacitus Cicero prætereare mihi ?
> Quod Flacco Varoq̧, fuit / summoq̧ Maroni
>   Mœcenas atauis regibus ortus eques !
> Id mihi ! si tenues non essent carmine uires !
>   Nunc fores eloquii diue pater Cicero ;
> Quem si cephaleis vulgaribus annotaui
>   His libris ! ueniam lector humane dabis !
> Hos quoq̧ quom legeris, precium ne (quæso) relinquas
>   Artificum ingenuæ quod meruere manus.
> Pro quibus optandi si nunc copia adesset !
>   Tam bene promeritis comoda mille precer ;

End. Fo. 87ª, line 6 :

> Quicquid Socraticæ manauit ab ordine sectæ !
> Quicquid Aristoteles docuit ! tuq̧ diuine Plato !
> Inuentum quodcunq̧ tuo Crisippe recessu !
> Quicquid Democritus risit ! dixitq̧ tacendo
> Pithagoras ! vno se pectore cuncta uetustas
> Condidit ! & maior Ciceronis uiribus exit !

His & enim libris docuit cognoscere ! curnam (*sic*)
Ipsa quidem uirtus precium sibi ! solaq̨ late
Fortunæ secura nitet ! nil indiga laudis
Externæ ! nec quærat opem ! ferat omnia secum !
Diuitiis animosa suis ! immotaq̨ cunctis
Casibus / exalta mortalia respuat arce.
Hanc tamē haud quisq̨ / qui non agnoscerit ante
Semet ! & incertos animi placauerit æstus
Inueniet. longis illuc ambagibus itur ;

[2 lines blank]

    Vale lector Studiose ;

Fo. 87ᵇ blank ; Fo. 88 entirely blank.

WATERMARK : Anchor.

REMARKS : The following pen corrections are found in most of the copies : in the first piece of Erhard, Fo. 86ᵇ, verse 5, *Varo* altered from *Vano* wrongly printed, *Maroni* instead of *Marconi*, also printed by mistake of the compositor ; in the second piece, Fo. 87ᵃ, verse 13, *tamen* and *haud* are corrected.

COPIES KNOWN : John Rylands Library, Manchester ; Bibliothèque Nationale, Paris, 2 copies, one bound with the *De Officiis*, the other imperfect ; Bibliothèque de Bourges ; Bibliothèque de Toulouse, **bound with the** *De Officiis*, Count Hoym's copy ; University Library, Basel, Heynlin's copy, followed by the *De Officiis* of Cicero and the *De Officiis* of St. Ambrosius, bound in the same volume.

XIII. RODERICUS, SPECULUM HUMANÆ VITÆ. 1472. **Fol.**

COLLATION : [a-e¹⁰ ; f-g⁸ ; h-o¹⁰ ; p⁸] no printed signatures or catchwords ; 142 ff., 32 ll.

REGISTER : *a* 1ᵃ, Ad sanctissimū ; *b*, cernamus ; *c*, nem ! quū ; *d*, ritos ; *e*, ritatē ; *f*, tes & ; *g*, cēdi ars ; *h*, imppetuū ! ; *i*, incipit ; *k*, plurimis ; *l*, Ca. ix : *m*, thesaurarius ; *n*, Gregorius ; *o*, monastica ! ; *p*, uantiā.

DESCRIPTION : Fo. 1ᵃ, Ad sanctissimū & beatissimū dominū / dominū Paulū ‖ Secundū Pontificē Maximū ! liber incipit dictus Spe- ‖ culum humanæ uitæ (Quia in eo cuncti mortales in ‖ quouis fuerint statu uel officio spirituali aut tpali ! ‖ speculabunt eius artis & uitæ prospera & aduersa ! ac ‖ recte uiuēdi documenta) editus a Rodorico zamorensi & postea Calagaritano hispano / eiusdē sanctitatis in ‖ castro suo Sancti Angeli castellano ; Fo. 2ᵇ, line 16, Prefatio utilis ! in qua autoris huius libri / vita ! eiusq̨ ‖ studia recolunt. & tandem admouet ad studia legis di- ‖ uinę potius q̄ humanæ. & de effectu legum humanarum ‖ & de ordine procedendi in hoc libro ; Fo. 4ᵇ, line 12, De materiis pertractandis in primo libro. & de tabu ‖ la capitulorum **eius** ; Fo. 9ᵃ, Incipit capitulū primū p̄mi libri ! uidelicet de primo & ‖ **sublimiori** statu tēporali ! qui est status & gradus impi ‖ alis & regalis **ac** alioR, p̄ncipum sæcularium. & de sup̄- ‖ mo huius status & dignitatis culmie & exellētia (*sic*) ! ac de ‖ illius gł̄a & fœlicitate laudibɔ & p̄coniis sup alias tp̄ales dignitēs ; Fo. 75ᵃ, line 29 blank, line 30, Einit (*sic*) Liber primus ! de ōni statu & statu & uita tēporali ; Fo. 75ᵇ blank ; Fo. 76 blank ; Fo. 77, line 1, Incipit Liber Secundus ! de Statu & Vita ‖ Spirituali / ecclesiastica & Regulari ; Fo. 137ᵇ [line 20 blank], line 21 :

> Edidit hoc linguæ clarissima norma **latinæ** !
> Excelsi ingenii uir Rodoricus opus.
> Qui norma angelica est custos bene fidus **in arce** !
> Sub Pauli ueneti nomine pontificis.
> Claret in Italici Zamorensis episcopus ausis
> **Eloquii** ! it superos gloria parta uiri ;

Fo. 138ᵃ, Incipit Repertorium siue Tabula per alphabetum ‖ ad faciliter recipiendas materias in pręsenti libro ‖ Dicto Speculum Humanæ uitæ ; *End.* Fo. 141ᵃ [line 16 blank], line 17, Finis foelix atq͛, optatus illius breuis ‖ tabulæ siue repertorii per alphabetū / ‖ in pręsentem libR ! speculum humanæ uitæ nuncupatum ; Fo. 141ᵇ **blank** ; Fo. 142 blank.

WATERMARKS : None.

REMARKS : The copy preserved in the British Museum contains at the end of the volume three letters not included in our description, and addressed by the printers : **1°.** to Robert d'Estouteville, provost of Paris : Magnifico militi domino Roberto de Estoteuille ‖ pręposito Parisiensi / et christianissimi francoR, regis Cambellario / impressores Parisienses se ipsos perpetuo seruituros / humiliter offerunt ; **2°.** to Jean de Bourbon, **Duke of** Auvergne ; this begins : Inuictissimo p̄ncipi Iohanni bourbonii atq͛, aluernię duci ! ‖ comiti Claromontēsi, forensi insulæq͛, Iordani d̄no belli io- ‖ ci. pari atq͛, camerario franciæ libroR, Parisii **impressores** ‖ germani / sese perpetuo seruituros liberalissime offerunt ; **3°. to the** King Louis XL, dated at the end, **Tua** in Lutetia x kal. maii Anni millesimi quadringentesimi secundi ‖ supra septuagesimū ! manibus tibi deditissimoR, Martini Vdal ‖ rici atq͛, Michaelis impressum, and subscribed, Christianissimo francoR, regi diuo Ludouico quarto (*sic*) ‖ Germani libroR, impressores Parisienses / perpetuo ‖ se deuouent seruituros. These letters, printed for special presentation copies, do not exist in the other copies known.

COPIES KNOWN : British Museum ; Bibliothèque Nationale, Paris, 3 copies ; Bibliothèque de Bordeaux ; Bibliothèque de Rodez ; University Library, Basel, 2 copies, Heynlin's copy, and another dated 1473 by the rubricator ; Imperial Library, Vienna ; Duke d'Aumale's Library, Chantilly.

XIV. PLATONIS EPISTOLÆ. N. D. 4°.

COLLATION : [a-d¹⁰ ; e⁸ ; f²] no printed signatures or catchwords ; 50 ff., 23 ll.

REGISTER: *a* 1ª, Ad prudentem ; *b*, ruisses ! longe ; *c*, sitati scimus ; *d*, qui ad reperiendũ ; *e*, detur) malo ; *f*, pulo uenirem.

DESCRIPTION: Fo. 1ª blank ; Fo. 2ª, Ad prudentem & magnificum uirum ∥ Cosmã de medicis florentinũ / Leonardi ∥ Aretini clarissimi oratoris / in epłas pła ∥ tołs quas ex gręcis latinas fecit ! p̃fatio ; *End.* Fo. 50ᵇ, line 15, FINIS. [Lines 16 and 17 blank.] Line 18 :

    Discite rectores / diuinitus / ore platonis !
    Quid uos / qd ciues reddat in urbe bonos.

WATERMARKS : A pot or jug ; a stag's head with a **cross between the** antlers ; **a kind** of ox head with a cross between the **horns ; an anchor with** a small cross in the middle at the top.

REMARKS : Philippe reckons two blank leaves at the beginning. This is a mistake ; they are independent flyleaves.

COPIES KNOWN : Bibliothèque d'Angers ; University Library, Basel (Heynlin's copy) ; another copy quoted in the Crevenna catalogue, its whereabouts unknown.

XV. PHALARIDIS, BRUTI ET **CRATIS** EPISTOLÆ. N. D. 4°.

COLLATION : a-e¹⁰ ; f⁸ ; g¹⁰ ; h-i⁹ ; no printed signatures or **catchwords** ; 82 ff., 23 ll.

REGISTER : *a* 1ª, Francisci ; *b*, sarias VeR ; *c*, eum ꝓolamini ! ; *d*, ex parte ; *e*, eoR, liberoR, ; *f*, imicos p̃bamus ; *g*, Raimitii ; *h*, remitterē ! ; *i*, & intēperantiam !

DESCRIPTION : Fo. 1ª, Francisci Aretini ! phalaridis agrigentini ∥ in epistolas / ad illustrem principem malatestã ∥ nouellum de malatestis ! prohemium incipit ; Fo. 56ᵇ, last line, EpistolaR, Phalaridis fœlix finis ; Fo. 57ª, **Raimitii ! in catalogum** Mitridatis de epi- ∥ stolis .M. bruti ad Nicolaũ quintũ ponti- ∥ ficem maximum ! præfatio fœliciter incipit ; Fo. 73ª, line 23, Catalogus epłaR, bruti finit fœliciter ; Fol. 73ᵇ [the first half of the page blank, the other half with nine printed lines], Epigramma in catalogũ epłaR, Cratis ∥ cynici / Diogenis discipuli ;

    Hæ tibi uirtutũ stimulos / & semina laudũ /
    Atq̃, exēpla dabũt cynicæ / o lector studiose.
    Pieriis etenim studiis / multoq̃, redundant
    Eloquio ! ne desidiis / dapibus ue paratis
    Indulgere uelis ! ue ignaua & marcida luxu
    Ocia / ne torpens somnos admittere inertes
    Discere sed quantũ paupertas sobria possit ;

Fo. 74ª, **Atanasius** Constantinopolitanus / ∥ archiensis abbas / ad diuum p̃ncipem ∥ **Karolum** Aragonum / p̃mogenitum ; *End.* Fo. 82ᵇ, line 8, Finis

CynicaR, Cratis ; ‖ Erhardi Vuinsberg Epigrāma ad ger- ‖ manos librarios
egregios / michaelem / mar ‖ tinum atq̃, udalricum ;

 Plura licet summæ dederi alemannia laudi !
  At reor hoc maius te genuisse nihil.
 Q̃ prope diuinā summa ex industria fingis
  Scribendi hanc artem multiplicans studia.
 Fœlices igit̃ Michael / Martineq̃, semper
  Viuite / & Vlrice ! hoc q̃s opus imprimit̃.
 Erhardum uestro & nõ dedignemini amore !
  Cui fido semper pectore clausi eritis ;

WATERMARK : Crowned fleur-de-lys with letter J at end.

REMARKS : In one of the copies of the Bibliothèque Nationale the word *Alemannia*, in the first verse of Erhard Windsberg's epigram, is altered with the pen to *Argentina*. No such correction is to be found in the other copies. It is a forgery made up at the suggestion of Mentel, an historian of typography, in the seventeenth century. Philippe (p. 144) says that the verses of Erhard Windsberg in the copy of the Bibliothèque Mazarine are placed after the letters of Brutus, instead of being placed at the end. This is a mistake. The verses seen by Philippe are the same as the verses preceding the letters of Crates in all the copies, and are not the distichs alluding to the new industry of printing.

COPIES KNOWN : British Museum ; John Rylands Library, Manchester ; Bibliothèque Nationale, Paris [2 copies] ; Bibliothèque Mazarine, Paris [the letters of *Brutus* only] ; University Library, Basel [Heynlin's copy; the letters of *Phalaris* are placed at the end] ; Cantonal Library, Luzern [Erhard Windsberg's copy, bound with the *Orations* of Bessario ; Imperial Library, Vienna ; Library of the late Duke d'Aumale, Chantilly.

XVI. VIRGILIUS MARO (PUBLIUS). BUCOLICA & GEORGICA. N. D. 4°.

COLLATION : [a^{12}; b-d^{10} ; e^8] no printed signatures or catchwords ; 50 ff., 32 ll.

REGISTER : *a* 2^a, Publii Virgilii ; *b*, Ducite ; *c*, Deniq̃, quid ; *d*, Vel scena ; *e*, Verum ubi.

DESCRIPTION : Fo. 1, entirely blank ; Fo. 2^a, Publii Virgilii maronis mantuani uatis clarissimi ‖ Bucolica & Aegloga prima fœliciter incipit. ‖ [1 line space] ‖ Hic deflet melibœus pfugiat quid inique. ‖ Tityrus ast lætus quis contulit otia dicit ; ‖ *End.* Fo. 50^a, line 28, Illo Virgilium me tempore dulcis alebat ‖ Parthenope ! studiis florentem ignobilis oti. ‖ Carmina qui lusi pastorum. audaxq̃, iuuenta ‖ Tityre te patule cecini sub tegmine fagi ; ‖ Finis fœlix GeorgicoR, Virgilii. ‖ ; Fo. 50^b blank.

WATERMARKS : Shield with three fleurs-de-lys with the letter t below ; letter y, or rather a gothic P with a curved tail, and a small cross above, as in the *Sophologium* (see No. XXI. below).

COPIES KNOWN : John Rylands Library, Manchester.

XVII. JUVENALIS ET PERSII SATYRÆ. N. D. Fol.

COLLATION: [a–c¹⁰; f¹²] no printed signatures or catchwords; 74 ff., 32 ll.

REGISTER: *a* 1ᵃ, Decimi; *b*, Si rixa; *c*, In quo; *d*, Sanguine; *e*, Sit licet; *f*, Arguit; *g*, Auli.

DESCRIPTION: Fo. 1ᵃ, Decimi Iunii Iuuenalis Satyrar̄ ‖ Liber primus. ‖ Materiā & causam satyrar̄ hac inspice prima. ‖ Fo. 61ᵇ, line 25, Decimi Iunii Iuuenalis Aquinatis ‖ Satyrarum liber finit Fœliciter; ‖ Erhardus / D. I. Iuuenal' cultori. F. optat;

   Ecce parens satyrar̄ / princeps eliconis et auctor !
   In prauos mittens tela seuera notæ.

Fo. 62 blank; **Fo. 63ᵃ, Auli persii flacci in** satyrar̄ librum prolo- ‖ gus constans metro iambico trimetro; *End.* **Fo.** 73ᵇ, line 20, A. P. F. Satyrar̄ liber finit fœliciter. ‖ Erhardi Tetrastichon **ad germanos** ‖ librarios ingenuos.

   Ecce tibi princeps satyror̄ codice paruo
   Persius ! arte noua impressus ! & ingenue.
   Fœlices igit̄ alemannos ! arte magistra
   Qui studia ornantes / sertis in astra gradum ;

Fo. 74 blank.

WATERMARK: Anchor.

REMARKS: The tetrastich **to** the printers by Erhard Windsberg **at the** end of the *Persius* is not to be found in the copy at Avignon. The **space** occupied by these verses in other copies is blank here.

COPIES KNOWN: Magdalen College, Oxford; John Rylands Library, Manchester; Bibliothèque d'Avignon; University Library, Basel (Heynlin's copy), bound with the *Terence*.

XVIII. TERENTIUS. N. D. Fol.

COLLATION: [a–h¹⁰; i⁶] **no** printed signatures or catchwords; **86 ff.,** 32 ll.

REGISTER: *a* 1ᵃ, Publii Terentii afri; *b*, Sat **habeo**; *c*, **Forte habui**; *d*, Argumentum; *e*, quā rem agis; *f*, to omnē **ordine**; *g*, **Parmeno seruus**; *h*, tantū ne est ?; *i*, Sed mihi opus.

DESCRIPTION: Fo. 1ᵃ, Publii Terentii afri poetę comici Andria incipit fœliciter. ‖ Ephitaphium Terentii. ‖ Natus in excelsis tectis cartaginis alte ‖ Romanis ducibus bellica preda fui. ‖ Descripsi mores hominum, iuuenumq̄ ‖ senumq̄ ! ‖ Qualiter & serui decipiant dominos. ‖ Quid meretrix ! quid leno dolis confingat auarus. ‖ Hæc quicunq̄ legit ! sic puto cautus erit ; ‖ [etc.] leaf 86ᵇ, line 21, ad cœnā uoca. Nau. Pol uero uoco. De. eamus intro hinc. Chre. ‖ **Fiat.** sed ubi est phedria iudex noster ? Phor. Iam hic faxo ! ad- ‖

erit; Valete, & plaudite. Caliopius recensui; ‖ [1 line space] ‖ Publii Terenti Afri Poætæ Comici ‖ ComœdiaR liber Finit Fœliciter; ‖

WATERMARK: None.

COPIES KNOWN: John Rylands Library, Manchester; Bibliothèque Nationale, Paris (copy formerly belonging to Grosley of Troyes, imperfect); University Library, Basel (Heynlin's copy, bound with the *Juvenal* and *Persius*); an imperfect copy advertised in a catalogue of Baer, 282, No. 1083, Frankfort on Main, 1892.

XIX. ÆNEAS SYLVIUS, DE DUOBUS AMANTIBUS. N. D. 4°.

COLLATION: [a-d¹⁰; e⁶] no printed signatures or catchwords; 46 ff., 23 ll.

REGISTER: *a* 1ᵃ, Aeneæ; *b*, non nunq̄; *c*, Cauponē; *d*, tur herus!; *e*, test ex causa.

DESCRIPTION: Fo. 1ᵃ, Aeneæ siluii poætæ (*sic*) laureati / in hystoriā ‖ de duobus amātibus p̄fatio prima ad per / ‖ q̄ generosum militē Casparem Slik fœli- ‖ citer incipit; *End*. Fo. 44ᵇ, line 9, Aeneę Siluii poętę laureati de duobus ‖ amātibus eurialo & lucresia finit fœlicit; Fo. 45 and 46 blank.

WATERMARK: None.

COPIES KNOWN: Bibliothèque Nationale, Paris; Bibliothèque Mazarine, Paris; Bibliothèque de Rouen; Imperial Library, Vienna.

XX. ÆNEAS SYLVIUS, DE CURIALIUM MISERIA. N. D. 4°.

COLLATION: [a-c¹⁰; d⁶] no printed signatures or catchwords; 36 ff., 23 ll.

REGISTER: *a* 1ᵃ, Aeneæ; *b*, us infinitos; *c*, inicio mēsæ; *d*, est difficile.

DESCRIPTION: Fo. 1ᵃ, Aeneæ Siluii poætæ (*sic*) laureati (cui & pro ‖ pontificali dignitate Pio nomen est) in ‖ disputationē de curialiū miseria / ad per: ‖ spicacissimū iurisconsultū Iohannē Ech / ‖ serenissimi / diuiq̄ principis / Alberti / cæ- ‖ saris inuictissimi! Alberti quoq̄ austriæ ‖ ducis inclyti consiliariū atq̄ oratorē præ- ‖ facio fœliciter incipit; *End*. Fo. 34ᵃ, line 13, Aeneæ Siluii de curialium miseria di- ‖ sputatio finem habet fœlicem; Fo. 34ᵇ blank; Fo. 35 and 36 blank.

WATERMARK: None.

REMARKS: Fo. 29ᵃ, one line omitted by the printer. It is written at the foot of the page after line 23, *nō te uolunt. Quidā nō potentes sūt! ac ex.* In the copy of the Bibliothèque Mazarine the abbreviations differ slightly, *Nō te uolūt. Quidā nō potentes sūt! ac ex.*

COPIES KNOWN: Bibliothèque Nationale, Paris (2 copies); Bibliothèque Mazarine, Paris; University Library, Basel [Heynlin's copy]; Royal Library, The Hague.

XXI. Sophologium Jacobi Magni. N. D. Fol.

COLLATION: [a-x¹⁰; y⁸] no printed signatures or catchwords; 218 ff., 32 ll., and sometimes only 31 ll.

REGISTER: *a* 1ª, Sequit́; *b*, Vñ seneca; *c*, toricā; *d*, Capitulum sextum; *e*, honestū est; *f*, perpenderūt; *g*, scilicet; *b*, pulchra est; *i*, ualerius; *k*, sæpe; *l*, fuerat; *m*, q̱ boni; *n*, Capitulum undecimum; *o*, habeant!; *p*, quæ impudicæ; *q*, id est; *r*, Qui igit̄; *s*, clementissimus; *t*, Capitulum tricesimum!; *u*, in milite; *x*, ad italiā; *y*, Capitulum tredecimum!

DESCRIPTION: Fo. 1ª, Sequit̄ tabula capitulorum istius libri. ‖ Et primo capitula primi libri; Fo. 4ª, Doctissimi atq̱ excellentissimi patris ! sacraR, litteraR, ‖ doctoris deuotissimi ! fratris Iacobi magni ! religionis ‖ fratrum HeremitaR, ! sancti Augustini Sophologium ‖ incipit. Cuius principalis intentio est inducere legē ‖ tis animum ad sapientiæ amorem; Fo. 217ª [line 31 blank], line 32:

    Iacobi magni Sophologium finit foeliciter;

End. Fo. 217ᵇ:

    Epigramma ad huius operis conspectorem;
        [Second line blank.]
    Istuc clarorum contendunt dogmata patrum !
        Doctos atq̱ bonos / ut faciant homines.
    At quom non leuiter possit percurrere quisquam /
        Auctores cunctos ! multa neglecta manent.
    Omnia doctoR, quo ergo documenta legantur !
        Hunc Iacobus magni / condidit ecce librum.
    Tu quoq̱ si bonus esse uelis / sapiensq̱ uideri !
        Quod manibus tractas / disce Sophologium.
    Quicquid enim ueterum tetigit præceptio digna /
        Mille uoluminibus ! clauditur hoc opere;

Fo. 218 entirely blank.

WATERMARK: Letter y, or rather a gothic P, with a curved tail and a small cross at the top; crowned fleur-de-lys, with the letters J. B. at end.

REMARKS: In some copies, Fo. 4ª, last line, *linguis* is corrected to *regnis*; Fo. 29ª, line 7, *conueniat* is corrected to *contineat*; Fo. 187ᵇ, a line of text passed over by the printers is written by hand at the foot of the page, *qssima ingenia haberet. maluert̄ suis moribȝ ⚹ legibȝ*; Fo. 191ª, line 31, *inimicus* is corrected to *inuictus*; Fo. 217ᵇ, second verse, *faciunt* is corrected to *faciant*.

COPIES KNOWN: Bodleian Library, Oxford; Bibliothèque Nationale, Paris; Bibliothèque Ste. Geneviève, Paris, 2 copies (both imperfect); Bibliothèque de Besançon; Bibliothèque de Tours; Bibliothèque de Caen; Bibliothèque de Bourges; Bibliothèque de St. Brieuc; Bibliothèque d'Aix;

Bibliothèque de Grenoble; Bibliothèque de Bordeaux; Bibliothèque de Nice; Bibliothèque de Rodez; Bibliothèque de Colmar; University Library, Breslau.

XXII. AMBROSIUS, DE OFFICIIS, ET SENECA, DE IV VIRTUTIBUS. N. D. Fol.

COLLATION: [a-i¹⁰; k⁸] no printed signatures or catchwords; 94 ff., 32 ll.

REGISTER: *a* 1ᵃ, Ambrosii; *b*, stellæ; *c*, net personis; *d*, mansionem; *e*, egeret; *f*, uita; *g*, hominum; *h*, oculos; *i*, Otius huius; *k*, Senecæ.

DESCRIPTION: Fo. 1ᵃ, Ambrosii ecclesię doctoris sapientissimi / mediolanoR, pre- ‖ sulis sacratissimi / ad suos quos in christo per euangelium ‖ genuit filios carissimos / officioR, liber primus. In quo de ‖ honesto officiisq̇, a fontibus quattuor honesti exortis de- ‖ termināṡ / in quattuor partitus tractatus! fœliciī incipit; Fo. 90ᵇ, end of the page, Capitulum tertium huic operi finem imponens! qualiter ‖ beatus Ambrosius ex hoR, præceptoR, fructu & utilitate / ad ‖ hmōi in mente ɔseruanda filios suos exhortatur! explicit. ‖ Quæ quidem nos uelle custodire & perficere / donet / ad cuius ‖ laudem hæc scripta sunt Iesus christus morum præceptor bo- ‖ norum & scientiarum dominus; Fo. 90ᵇ blank; Fo. 91ᵃ, Senecæ moralis philosophi de quattuor ‖ uirtutibus libellus fœliciter incipit; *End.* Fo. 94ᵇ, line 18, blank, line 19, Prudentissimi Senecæ opusculum de ‖ quattuor uirtutibus, finit foeliciter.

WATERMARK: None.

REMARKS: In one of the copies of the Bibliothèque Nationale without the *Seneca*, Fo. 30ᵇ, a MS. line is added at the foot of the page to indicate an inversion of the binder, *māsionē Itaq̄ hiis totū codicē scȝ decē folia ad tlē sign⁹*†. Philippe makes two separate articles of the *Ambrosius* and the *Seneca*. Our opinion is that they form part of the same volume, and were printed to be united and go together.

COPIES KNOWN: Bibliothèque Nationale, Paris, 3 copies [one complete, and two others without the *Seneca*]; Bibliothèque Ste. Geneviève, Paris, 2 copies [one complete, having belonged to the library of the Monastery of St. Victor, the other without the *Seneca*, and wanting the table of chapters]; Bibliothèque de Rodez; University Library, Basel [Heynlin's copy].

DOCUMENTS.

DOCUMENTS.

I.

GASPARINI EPISTOLÆ.

Letter of Fichet to Jean de la Pierre.

Guillermus Fichetus parisiensis theologus doctor Ioanni Lapidano Sorbonensis scholæ priori salutem.

Misisti nuper ad me suauissimas Gasparini pergamensis epistolas, non a te modo diligenter emendatas, sed a tuis quoque germanis impressoribus nitide et terse transcriptas. Magnam tibi gratiam gasparinus debeat, quem pluribus tuis uigiliis ex corrupto integrum fecisti. Maiorem uero cætus doctorum hominum, quod non tantum sacris litteris (quæ tua prouincia est) magnopere studes, sed redintegrandis etiam latinis scriptoribus insegnem operam nauas, res sane te uiro doctissimo et optimo digna, ut qui cum laude et gloria sorbonico certamini dux prefuisti, tum latinis quoque litteris (quas ætatis nostræ ignoratio tenebris obumbrauit) tua lumen effundas industria. Nam præter alias complures litterarum grauiores iacturas, hanc etiam acceperunt ut librariorum uitiis effectæ pene barbaræ uideantur. At uero maxime lætor hanc pestem tua prouidentia tandem eliminari procul a parisiorum lutetia. Etenim quos ad hanc urbem e tua germania librarios asciuisti quam emendatos libros ad exemplaria reddunt, idque tute macto studio conaris, ut ne ullum quidem opus ab illis prius exprimatur quam sit a te, coactis exemplaribus multis, castigatum litura multa. Quare tibi quæ carminum censori quintilio laus apud flaccum horatium merito debeatur, cum a gasparinea suaui facundia, tum a plerisque nobilibus huius ciuitatis ingeniis quæ, desputa barbaria, lacteum fontem eloquentiæ melle dulciorem degustant et indies quidem auidius. Ego uero (quod in aristotelis laudem dicebat plato) tuum domicilium lectoris studiosissimi sedem sine ulla quidem assentatione dici uelim.

Vale et me dilige te amantem. Scriptum apud sorbonam uelocissima fichetea manu.

II.

GASPARINI ORTHOGRAPHIA.

Letter of Fichet to Robert Gaguin, with the poetical answer of the latter.

Guillermus Fichetus Parisiensis theologus doctor Roberto Gaguino uiro doctissimo salutem.

Magna me uoluptas capit eruditissime Roberte, quum musas et omnes eloquentiæ partes (quas prior ætas ignorauit), in hac urbe florere conspicio. Nam ut me primum adolescentibus annis boico ex agro luteciam contuli (idque Aristoteleæ disciplinæ causa), mirabar sane oratorem aut poetam phœnice rariorem lutecia tota inueniri. Nemo Ciceronem (uti plerique nunc faciunt) nocturna uersabat manu, uersabat diurna. Nemo carmen fingebat legitimum, nemo fictum ab alio cæsuris nouerat librare suis. Desuefacta siquidem a latinitate schola parisiensis ad sermonis rusticitatem omnis pene deciderat. At lapillo longe meliore dies nostri numerantur, quippe quibus di, deæ que omnes (ut poete loquuntur) benedicendi artes indies magis magisque aspirant. Siquidem (ut missos faciam alios) tu usque adeo musis et omni carminis genere præstas, ut si non solum illi quidem uates nobilissimi (tibulus, Lucretius, Horatius, Naso, Statius, Lucanus, Marcialis, Persius, Iuuenalis), sed etiam longe princeps Virgilius, ab heliseis campis ad nos remearent, profecto tuum carmen suum arbitrarentur. Quid enim Maroni tuo carmine similius quod de Ludouico rege nostro fortissimo proximis diebus cecinisti? Quid illo quadratius, quod dialogorum instar unum aut alterum effinxisti? Tacceo ciuitatis pariseæ laudes quæ adeo sunt a te uerborum uenustate et sentenciarum grauitate referte, ut utrum utri laude preferatur iudicare sit difficile. Pretereo quæ de galliæ hyspaniæque prestantia soluta oratione scripsisti. Non enim est huius temporis de tuis studiis presertim ad te scribere. De studiorum humanitatis restitutione loquor. Quibus (quantum ipse coniectura capio) magnum lumen nouorum librariorum genus attulit quos nostra memoria (sicut quidam equus troianus) quoquo uersus effudit germania. Ferunt enim illic, haut procul a ciuitate Maguncia, Ioannem quendam fuisse cui cognomen bonemontano, qui primus omnium impressoriam artem excogitauerit, qua non calamo (ut prisci quidem illi) neque penna (ut nos fingimus) sed æreis litteris libri finguntur, et quidem expedite, polite et pulchre. Dignus sane hic uir fuit quem omnes musæ, omnes artes, omnesque eorum linguæ qui libris delectantur, diuinis laudibus ornent, eoque magis dis deabusque anteponant, quo propius ac presentius litteris ipsis ac studiosis hominibus suffragium tulit. Si quidem deificantur liber et alma ceres, ille quippe dona liei inuenit poculaque inuentis acheloia miscuit uuis, hæc chaoniam pingui glandem mutauit arista. Atque (ut poeta utamur altero) prima ceres unco glebam dimouit aratro, prima dedit fruges alimentarmitia terris. At bonemontanus ille, longe gratiora diuinioraque inuenit, quippe qui litteras **ciusmodi** exculpsit quibus quidquid dici aut cogitari potest, propediem scribi ac transcribi et posteritatis mandari memoriæ possit. Neque presertim hoc loco nostros silebo, qui superant iam arte magistrum, quorum Vdalricus, Michael ac Martinus principes esse dicuntur, qui iam pridem Gasparini pergamensis epistolas impresserunt, quas ioannes lapidanus emendauit, quin illius auctoris orthographiam (quam hic etiam accurate correxit) se accingunt perficere, opus mea quidem sentencia egregium, neque auribus solum iuuentutis gratissimum sed doctiorum quoque studiis oportunum. Non enim (quod pace multorum dictum esse uelim) res est orthographia fructu paruo ac tenui, verum pergrandi, gratissimo, apprime necessario et iocundo. Si quidem **recte** scribendi ratio (quam o[r]thographiæ sonat interpretatio) nobis in omni lingua, greca, latina, uernaculaque suffragatur; qua sine nil emendate ac pure scribi, nil legi, nil nisi contorte efferri possit. Quotum enim quenque, siue grammaticum, siue oratorem, **siue** philosophum excelluisse inuenias, qui non huic diuinæ arti maiorem in modum studuerit? Nempe (ut hinc incipiam) didimus cum omnem, tum hanc grammatice partem libris quamplurimis exornauit, quo fit ut omnibus artis grammaticæ professoribus (qui quidem essent ac fuissent) Macrobius eum jure protulerit. Nigidius (quoque cui figulo fuit cognomen) auli Gelii sentencia secundum Marcum Varronem locum est consecutus. Cur ita? nimirum quia multus in orthographiæ præceptione fuisset. Quid Anthonius empho? Profecto tantus huic est habitus honos, uel ab ipso marco cicerone, ut etiam illius scholam post exactum forensem laborem hic **studiose** frequentaret. Igini quoque grammatici magnum fuit in exponenda recte scribendi scientia studium, utpote qui rome multa scripsit et docuit. Sed (ne forte in re tritissima sim longior) mitto Valerium probum, scaulum, anneum, cassellium, terentium, cornutum et alios illius superioris ætatis quam plurimos qui et ipsi gram**matici et** recte scribendi studiosi fuerunt. Proximiores et minus antiquos non dicam dyomedem, donatum, seruium, uictorinum quos equidem grammaticos ne an philosophos potissimum **dicam nescio**. Illud certo scio, non grammaticen modo sed et rhetoricen et philosophiam eximiæ laudi omnibus fuisse. Verum (quando quidem oratores et philosophos incidimus) ex his paucos et principes testimonio nobis asciscimus. Marcus etenim tullius (quem principem suæ linguæ latinus quisque esse uoluit) non apposite tantum singula scripsit, sed et ipse quoque per epistolam filium ammonuit ut emendate scriptionis artem perdisceret. Caii cæsaris itidem extant de analogia **libri**. **Cuius** cæsaris? Eius qui cum in omni re maxima et forensi et bellica preter **cetera** gloriam perquesiuit, tum in hac parte una et maxima curiosissimus indagator esse uoluit, et quod uoluit attigit, et quod attigit cum forensibus bellicisque laudibus mandauit posteritati. Messale (cuius laudis causa meminit horacius) non impolitus litterarii ludi scriptor affloruit. Nam preter fori gloriam (qua ne par quidem in quo quam æquali suo fuit) scite scribendi precepta conscripsit quin de nonnullis litteris integros libros confecit. Marcum etiam uarronem (quem sine dubitatione doctissimum cicero dixit) ex hac doctrina ingens gloria secuta est, et eo quidem ingentior quo rem omnem altius fodieando funditus pertigit. De C. basso, fabio quintiliano plinioque tacere consilium est, qui non minus propter hanc (de qua loquimur) scribendi sapientiam sapientissimi sunt habiti quam ob eloquentiam et alias artes multas et bonas quibus eorum quisque excelluit. Sed ego quid oratores philosophosque commemorem? Utique in hoc genere laudis infiniti succurrunt memoriæ, quos non nisi inuitus prætereo. Prætereo papirianum, qui superioris cuiusque præcepta unum in opus artificiose contexuit. Aulus etiam Gelius ommittatur cuius tantus in hac re fuit conatus, immo superfuit, ut ab eo nullæ uel minutissimæ fibre relinquantur intacte. Aequalis gelii fauorinus sileatur, quem doctissimum fuisse scribere gelius haut dubitauit. Neque sergius, neque herodianus, neque latinis quisquam siue grammaticus, siue orator, siue philosophus a me deinceps dicatur. Quid de græcis inquies? Vereor ne fortassis eorum fontes illibatos preteriens non degustatione dignos uidear iudicasse, contraque si uel extremis labris attigero præter modum euagari ac nescio si rectius dicam debacchari uideatur oratio. Itaque modestie malim quam loquendi licentiæ morigerari ne si uel aristotelis, uel theodectis, uel porphirii, uel appollonii (qui gloriosissime hanc etiam partem aspexerunt) uelim exemplis nos hortari, ipsa uerborum longitudine potius ipse dehorter. Quas ob res abunde colliquescit quod inicio constitui, neminem unquam, uel de grammaticis, uel de rhetoricis uel philosophorum institutis bene meritum extitisse qui non magnopere scribendi doctrine incumberet. Neque aliunde plures errores, ne grauiores quidem, in litteris, in poetis, oratoribus, hystoria, medicinis, iure ciuili, sacris litteris, quauis denique philosophie particula crediderim emersisse quam ex unius orthographie et appositæ scriptionis ignoratione. Quocirca magis ætatis nostræ quam superiori quidem illi congratulor, quin quidem uideo cum studiis, tum libris artificiose scribendi dicendique scientia assecutum iri quamplurimos, neque nomen (quod longe lateque uolitet per orbem) defore quibusque nostris hominibus, modo ipsi sibi non prius defuerint. Vale et epistole longitudinem tribue amori nostro quam maximo. Aedibus sorbone raptim a me Kalendis Ianuariis diluculo scriptum.

Eiusdem doctoris in superiorem epistolam metrica superscriptio.

  Iane pater, ferto nunc munera nostro Roberto,
  Vni qui musis fœlix eat omnibus æuis.

Patri et preceptori suo guillermo ficheto theologo doctori, Robertus Gaguinus de ordine sanctæ trinitatis et captiuorum salutem plurimam dicit.

  Quos luteos homines finxit natura **deauras**,
  Et facis eloquio, clare fichete, deos.
  Te digne extulerit preclara lutetia cælo,
  Cui tua rectiloquos lingua diserta parit.
  Quæ fuit obscura sterili ruditate loquendi,
  Fulgida nunc radiis arte polita micat.
  Puluerulenta situ et squalore **uolumina longo**
  Exiliunt tenebris en reuoluta suis.
  Per cathedras Cicero uerbi pater intonat acer,
  Et ueterum mille nomina lecta uirum.
  Quos equidem (si sensa animos retinere putandum est)
  Gratari inter se, nunc tibi (crede) iuuat.

Magnum autem est fama, et pulchrum memorarier actis,
Quæ probet et celum quisque leuetur humo.
Qui ueniet post hac puro sermone latinus
Esse tuis domitum se feret auspiciis,
Inque sacros aditus (quod semper græcia fecit)
Dicendi appinget philosophia decus.
Ergo eris in nostris quod achiuis ille prometheus,
Qui terræ obstrictos igniit arte uiros;
Siue opifex hominum, qui duris cotibus auras
Indidit, illa iubens uiuere deucalion.
Gaude igitur doctor habiturus nomen in æuum,
Gaguinumque magis usque benignus ama.

                      Vale. Ex Maturinis primo die Ianuarii.

III.

BESSARIONIS ORATIONES.

Letter of presentation to Cardinal Rolin.

Reuerendissimo in Christo patri ac domino prestantissimo Ioanni Rolino episcopo Eduensi, tituli sancti Stephani in Celio monte presbitero cardinali, Guillermus Fichetus, parisiensis theologus. S. P. D. ac se ipsum offert humiliterque subicit.

Que sit erga Bessarionem Nicenum cardinalem tua beniuolentia, præstantissime pater, nequaquam sum nescius. Eas nanque laudes adhuc recenti memoria teneo quibus eum mihi tanquam sapientium seculi nostri facile principem predicabas, quom Edue Lucenaique mutuos, pro tua facilitate, de doctis hominibus sermones miscebamus. Quo fit ut opus eius (quo tuam prestantiam illius nomine dono) non dubitem auidissime te lecturum atque **tua** sponte que monet ille facturum. Sunt enim elegantissime quas in Turcum orationes edidit, **quarum** ad principes quidem nostros, religionum policiarumque rectores, mittendarum **mihi** munus imposuit, **et ea quidem** ratione ut illi pacem inter se concilient bellumque suscipiant aduersus **Turcorum gentem** longe superbissimam atque cruentissimam. Neque fore quicquam **ad** rem unam uel alteram explicandam gerendamque posset inueniri quod Bessario grauissime luculentissimeque non consequatur. Quod tute quidem legendo cogitandoque iudicabis, facturus etiam, uti firmissime credo, quicquid uel ad sedandos principes populosque christianos uel ad euertendum Turcorum imperium pertinebit. Vale, studiorum meorum educator et reliquorum (si que fortassis maiora succedent) excitator bonorum meorum magnificus.

Edibus Sorbone Parisii scriptum VIII. Kalendas maias.

IV.

FICHETI RHETORICA.

Letter of presentation to Cardinal Rolin.

Humanissimo patri Ioanni Rolino episcopo eduensi tituli Sancti Stephani in celio monte presbitero cardinali Guillermus fichetus alumnus eius S. P. D.

Spero pater excellentissime rhetoricum opus nostrum fore tibi iocundissimum. Non quia par tuis in me beneficiis sit, sed quia fructus est illorum ipsorum non ingratus, neque prius ulli, uel magis quam tibi debitus atque reddendus, qui glebæ mei ingenii (quæ duntaxat sementis inopia laborabat) opimum semen et sumptus amplissimos abhinc decennium ad hunc usque diem continuo suppeditasti, quo fit ut istinc merito tibi nascantur non tantum hi rhetorici mei commentarii, uerum etiam (si longiorem ætatem deus annuerit) in dies maturiora quædam. Tantum si quidem abest ut patiar satus a te mihi creditos arescere, ut etiam a me quotidie diligentius et propensius excolantur. Neque magis hoc facio ut sim tibi fruger quam ut uidear et sim quamgratissimus. Enimuero cæteri quemadmodum præstantie tuæ gratulentur aut gratum tibi faciant, ipsi uiderint. Ego uero non committam ut tantisper ingratus fuisse coarguar, dum breuissimo mortalis huius uitæ curriculo frui datur. Tibi uero si quid ex credito mihi tuo semine tuisque beneficiis fructus accesserit aut cæteris (exemplo tuo qui feracibus ingeniis beneficia sua fenerabunt) non mihi profecto referenda gratia est, sed ne habenda quidem, referatur autem rolinorum familie tuæque pietati, a qua nimirum hæc manasse dicentur omnia. Si quid tamen aliquando fichætea poterit industria, rolineas tuas laudes sæculorum omnium memoria longe lateque cognoscet. Vale parens alitorque mei ingenii.

Aedibus Sorbonæ, idibus iuliis scriptum, anno septuagesimo [uno] et quadringentesimo supra millesimum.

V.

FICHETI RHETORICA.

Letter of presentation to Guillaume Chartier, Bishop of Paris.

Excellentissimo patri domino Guillermo Quadrigario Parisiensi episcopo, Guillermus Fichetus Salutem plurimam dicit.

Si præ cæteris opusculo nouo (quod de rhetoricis institutionibus scripsi) te donare constitui, pater humanissime, uideor instituto meo quodam fecisse. Etenim cum omnibus uirtutibus me affectum esse cupiam, tum nihil est quod malim quam me & gratum esse & uideri, idque præcipue quidem apud te, qui non solum ecclesiastico beneficio (quo tempore studii parisiensis rectoratum gerebam) primus omnium munerasti, uerumetiam susceptis doctoralibus insignibus Parisii remorandi mihi tuo beneficio causa fuisti. Qua quidem in ciuitate si quid interea studiosis hominibus contulimus, siue theologiam mane, siue rhetoricam post meridiem pluribus annis quotidie docendo, uolo sit eorum iudicium qui merito tibi gratias proinde debeant, habeant & agant. Te uero duntaxat meæ qua sum in te uoluntatis mearumque lucubratiuncularum censorem esse uelim, quas fortassis in perscribendis oratoriis præceptis utilius & honestius consumpsimus quam plerique sæculo nostro faciunt, qui in multam noctem lucemque dormientes ad somnum escas & potum pecudum more nati uidentur, quin etiam feris bestiis eo deteriores quod eorum egregia studia lacerare impudentius pergunt, qui quod de nobilissimis artibus ingenue sentiunt in aliorum commoditatem scribendo docendoque largiuntur. Quos equidem perditissimos ueritatis hostes, nisi satius contemnendos quam formidandos iam dudum mihi persuasissem, a bene ceptis me sæpe deterruissent, neque profecto (de quo nunc facio tibi iudicandi potestatem), in hoc opere nostro, tuorum in me beneficiorum fructus extaret, neque de tuis in me clarissimis officiis posteritatem longius quicquam cognituram speraremus, quæ tamen (uti fore confido) non tam sine inuidia de meis uigiliis iudicabit quam de tuis mirificis operibus nunquam conticescet. Vale.

VI.

LAURENTIUS VALLA.

Letter of Senilis to Heynlin.

P. Paulus Senilis Ioanni Heynlin de Lapide salutem plurimam dicit.

Quom proximis diebus mecum ageres, uir humanitate litterisque excelens, ut clarissimi uiri Laurentii Vallæ, quem merito latinæ linguæ restauratorem dixerim, elegantias castigarem librariorum uitio corruptissimas, recepi tandem me id esse facturum, non quod ego me tanto oneri parem esse crediderim (quippe quod uix doctissimi homines ferre queant), sed quod tantum apud me auctoritas ualet ut fatear nihil a me tibi posse sine maxima ingratitudine denegari. Est profecto res ista & digna & pernecessaria, sed quæ doctum uirum & ociosum postulat, quorum mihi neutrum adesse tu optimus testis es. Nam & magnorum principum aulæ non ex imperitis literatos, sed ex literatis imperitos facere consuerunt. Et hæc procellosa tempora, non cartham aut calamum, sed equos sibi gladiumque deposcunt. Accedit etiam ad has difficultates quod ego in hanc urbem me furtim (ut ita dixerim) ob comparanda mihi quædam necessaria surripui, regem uersus illico rediturus. Inter has tamen tantas loci temporisque angustias gessi tibi morem ut potui melius & Laurentium nostrum non me ausim dicere emendasse, sed celerrime percurrisse, & quidem stomachabundum, tum quia non latini uiri, qualis ipse fuit, sed legere barbari hominis scripta uidebar, tum quia molestissimum mihi erat ad emendandos pro tenui ingeniolo meo tot librariorum errores omnino mihi otium denegari. Tuum igitur nunc officium est ut, posteaquam ego te iubente hoc negotium quod supra meas uires esse intelligo aggressus sum, tu optima lima tua tuoque grauissimo iudicio prosequaris plurima quæ adhuc corrigenda supersunt, ut ego agellum hunc spinis, lapidibus lolioque mundasse ac sarculo coluisse, tu uero plantis & uariorum florum genere exornasse iudiceris. Postulat hoc a te studiosorum iuuenum cœtus quibus hic liber maximæ utilitati futurus est; postulat Laurentius noster, qui quom ad extirpandam ab hominibus nostris hoc suo aureo libro barbariem incredibiles pene labores uigiliasque subierit, committendum non est ut nostra culpa ipse fuisse barbarus uideatur. Postulatque denique Senilis tui honor, in quem multos impetum facturos esse non dubito, præsertim in hac prestantissima urbe Lutetia, ubi nonnullos esse audio qui Ciceronis, latine linguæ omnium iudicio parentis, scripta castigent. Que res certe non mediocri mihi uoluptati est. Nam si forte ad me reprehendendum grauissimi censores isti descenderint, ego ad Ciceronem confugiam ut quo ipse olim urbem Romam a Catilina, eodem se meque ab istorum morsibus ense defendat. Vale.

P. Paulus Senilis cunctis bonarum litterarum cultoribus S. P. D.

> Rhetora quisquis amas, uates, linguamue latinam,
>   Laurenti hoc Vallæ perlege semper opus.
> Nanque docet uerum quo sunt sermone locuti
>   Tullius heroicum Virgiliusque pater.
> Et docet ut fuerunt uariis erroribus usi
>   Multi quos doctos inscia turba putat.
> Hunc igitur legito, iuuenis studiose senexque,
>   Si recte queris uerba latina loqui.

VII.

VALLÆ ELEGANTIÆ.

Letter of acknowledgment of Heynlin to Senilis.

Petro Paulo Senili christianissimi francorum regis secretario, Ioannes de Lapide S. P. D.

Etsi me iandudum multis officiis tibi deuinxeras, nunc tamen longe maioribus quom roganti mihi Laurentium Vallam (quem se uoluit semper haberi) quam emendatissimum quanquam latinissimum e corruptissimo barbarissimoque fecisti. Neque profecto uni mihi tantum beneficium cumulate dedisti, sed & omnibus eloquentiæ studiosis (qui quotidie multo plures quam ante Lutetiæ nascuntur), & ipsi quoque Laurentio, quem barbarum pene reddiderat ipsa librariorum barbaries. Quo fit ut fere nesciam a quo potissimum tibi gratiæ plures debeantur, a me ne cui morem gessisti, an a scholasticis parisiis quibus labor tuus fructum est allaturus quammaximum, an fortassis a Laurentio quem inde fere redemisti unde latinitatem uix tandem diuturnis laboribus pridem eripuisset, quemque non dubito (si quis modo suorum laborum est illi sensus post mortem) maiorem immodum (sic) tibi gratari, uelleque non impares tibi gratias atque sibi deberi, quorum alter latinitatem collapsam restaurauit, alter restauratorem ipsum simili pene ruina labentem impiger resarsit. Enimuero cæteri, ut quisque uolet, tibi Laurentioque gratias egerint, at ego tantas utrique me debere crediderim quantas Romulo Camilloque debet longa Romanorum posteritas, quorum alter urbem Romam primus exstruxit, alter postea delapsam primus restaurauit. Atque utinam ea mihi sit aliquando facultas quam pro mea uoluntate gratum tibi facere possim, qui mox a me rogatus tam frugerum laborem suscepisti, susceptum quoque consummasti. Neque sane quicquam reliquum fuit a me repertum a quo uel minutissimam scabram obtusa mea lima (quam deceptus amore optimam dixisti) posset excerpere, sed ne laurentianum quidem agrum tantum (ut scribis) spinis, lapidibus, lolioque mundasti & sarculo coluisti, uerumetiam (quod incassum mihi reliquum esse uoluisti) plantis & uario florum genere plurimum exornasti. Hec enim a me tantum abhorrent quantum uni tibi maxime sunt honori. Non enim ego (ut tu) in Latio, sed alias in Germania, alias Parisii, in nudo quodam & barbaro pene sermone florem ætatis consumpsi, neque tam oratoribus hic atque illic quam philosophis theologisque me addixi, indiesque magis addico, ut me uix quidem, si possem quod mones, Laurentio tuo liceret temporis punctum impartiri. Bene itaque mecum egisti qui usque adeo politum Laurentium reddidisti ut non a me, sed ne a se quidem, si uiueret, expolitior reddi posset. Obsequar tamen monitis tuis opera qua maxima potero, morem secutus quorundam famulantium qui, magna quom nequeant, in minimis quod summum ipsi habent libenter pollicentur ac faciunt. Laurentianum si quidem opus non solum singulis **capitulis** annotaui, sed unum (etiam uocabulum) quodque per alphabeti seriem in tabule modum distribui, quo quisque possit quod sibi uolet uocabulum sine labore desumere. Quæ res **si forte** cuiquam fuerit commoditati, non is mihi gratias habeat, at uero tibi quammaximas & agat & referat, qui me tuo beneficio tuisque litteris ut opere quiddam Laurentio prestarem obstrinxisti. Iam ergo nihil habeat noster Laurentius quod non merito tibi sit tribuendum, quem barbarorum faucibus eripuisti, quem sautium restaurasti, quem ad unguem politum nitidumque prodire iussisti, quem denique singulorum membrorum officiis distinctum in nostrorum hominum & omnis posteritatis usum longe lateque mandasti. Vale meque ama tui quidem amantissimum.

Aedibus Sorbone scriptum anno uno & septuagesimo quadringentesimoque **supra** millesimum.

VIII.

CICERO DE OFFICIIS.

Letter of presentation from Heynlin to George, Bishop of Metz.

Illustrissimo principi patrique in christo Reuerendo Domino Georgio Metensi Episcopo, Iohannes de lapide eius humillimus seruitor se ipsum offert atque donat.

Si, prestantissime pater, iocundissimum tue magnificentie meum munusculum fuerit, habeo suauissimum quem ex multis meis uigiliis fructum expecto. Quom enim doctor

Fichetus suis litteris mihi Ciceronis emendandos officiorum libros imposuisset, satisque fecissem (ut mihi quidem uidebar) hominis amicissimi preceptis tandem quod illi roganti concesseram existimaui, tue prestantiæ nequaquam roganti sed ne petenti quidem esse merito dicandum, offerendum atque tradendum. Tres itaque officiorum libros: Lelium, Catonem, Sextum de Re Publica, quos illius patris auctoritate promotus emendaui, capitulatimque distinxi, nunc tuæ illustrissimæ dominationi deuoueo. Est ne munus, excellentissime pater, quo nullum ad omnem uitæ rationem potius inuenias? Quippe mores non tam in summa quadam (ut Aristoteles quidem fecit) sed pro cuiusque gradu, etate, sexu, fortuna grauiter admodum et eleganter elucidat. Cuius lectio tum aures depascit, tum linguam expolit, tum ægritudines animi sanat omnes, tum bene beateque uiuendi fontem secludit et eo reficit ac faciat uniuersos. Quod experturam prestantiam tuam non dubito si legendi studio sepius in manibus hoc opus resumpserit. Quo circa rogatum te uolo, maioremque immodum obtestor, ut quod offero tibi munusculum hylari tuo uultu suscipias, eoque mentem et animum quotidie magis reficias, refectum ornes, ornatum illustres. Id quod scito certo fore tibi iocundissimum, qui non minus egregiis uirtutibus quam sanguine nobilissimo clarus euasisti. Vale *prestantissime pater*.[1]

IX.

CICERO DE OFFICIIS.

Letter of Fichet to Heynlin.

Guillermus fichætus parisiensis theologus doctor, Ioanni lapidano theologo professori S. P. D.

Multo familiarius quam omnibus fere quos in amicis recensui labores tibi impono. Vix enim quisquam posset inueniri qui sit erga me Lapidano meo beneuolentior aut litterario labore magis assiduus, aut officio (quod omnibus prosit) amantior. Proinde nequaquam subuereor ne forte neges te facturum quod pro multorum dignitate tuaque gloria per epistolam efflagito.

Nuper quom apud regem pro Gallorum principum concordia belloque contra Turcum obeundo Bessarionis Niceni cardinalis iussu uerba fecissem exitumque rerum mihi creditarum opperirer, inciderunt forte fortuna manus meas opera multa Ciceronis quæ Turonem externi quidam librarii (quos dicimus impressores) aduexerant. Eorum mihi lectio fuit in hoc curiali tumultu non ingrata, multoque iocundior quam quom eadem domi sepe sæpiusque legebam. Fuisset autem longe iocundissima si correctissimus et capitibus distinctissimus liber quisque fuisset quemadmodum Ciceronis orator, Valerius et Laurentius opera tua sunt impressi. Quibus distinctiones iste (capitula quæ nos appellamus) et ad cognitionem et ad memoriam magnum sane lumen recludunt, ut uel pueris eorum lectio sit aperta. Rogatum itaque te uolo ut Ciceronis officia (que parisienses librarii non longo post tempore sunt impressuri), prius isto

---

[1] The two words in italic are not printed, but written by Jean de la Pierre *propriâ manu*.

castigandi tuo distinguendique labore reddantur meliora. Est enim facillimus et iocundissimus uiro tibi doctissimo et officiosissimo labor futurus, ut cui nihil omnino **desit** quod istum laborem grauiorem tibi reddere possit: non diuinarum rerum contemplatio, qui theologice disputationis partes in Sorbona nostra longe primas attigisti, primusque nostra memoria parisii licentie munus ex theologis in Germanos transtulisti; non humanarum cognitio, qui philosophorum **ætatis quidem** nostre facile princeps euasisti; non usus rerum ciuilium, magister egregius qui **summum** schole parisiensis magistratum (quem rectoratum nominamus) prudentissime sapientissimeque gessisti. Taceo facultatis oratorie uim a qua ne tu quidem abhorres. Pretereo consuetum assiduumque laborem quippe qui litteris dies noctesque uehementer incumbis. Inde fructus multo etiam amplissimus omnes affluet. Officiorum nempe fonte diligenter aperto scituque purgato, singule mentis egritudines eius haustu mitigari diuellique poterunt facillime. Sapientia siquidem affectibus legem imponet, aequitati pristinus suus honos redibit, in suam se dignitatem animus attollet, nulla foris, ne domi quidem nos deseret moderatio. Ii uiri demum euademus quos Plotinus terrena penitus obliuisci celestia duntaxat meminisse fruique confirmat. Is quoque tibi post Ciceronem **erit honor** singularis qui post Aesculapium, Hippocrati Choo medicine restauratori longe clarissimo, aut Pisistrato post Homerum quem studiosius emendauit, aut Tucce Varoque post Maronem quibus nomen eternum promisit Aeneidis emendatio. Quin etiam tibi quam illis uia longe preclarior ad ueram laudem sua se sponte proponit. Aliarum si quidem artium elucidatio uix etiam attinet ad paucos atque cancellis angustissimis auctoris gloria contenta est, ceu Zenonis qui dialecticam, Tysie qui rhetoricam, Archimenidis, Euclidisue qui Geometriam, Phrimii qui Musicam, Athlantis qui Syderum cursus longe primus edocuit. Qui uero de uirtutibus & officiorum institutis aut ipsi scribunt aut aliorum ut tu scripta reparant quom in sinu, manibus, oculis & ore nobis semper obuertuntur, tum eorum nomen uel extra celum eternitatemque celebratum inuenias. Mittamus Moysem Israhelitis Pharoneum ægyptiis, Solonem atheniensibus, Licurgum spartanis, Numam Pompilium romanis quibus leges primus scripsit et edidit. Mittamus Socratem atque Ciceronem illum græcis, hunc latinis moratæ scientiæ doctorem aut certe primum aut in primis quidem egregium. Eorum dumtaxat paucos recenseo qui sunt in latinis ab ea disciplina quam legitimam dicunt. Apium dico Claudium, Sextum Hælium, Nasicam quidem illum cui cognomen senatus auctoritate inde fuit optimo, itemque Mutium propterea summum & uirum & ciuem appellatum, Seruium quoque Sulpitium cui legum emendatori Po. Ro. in legatione uita statuam pro rostris posuit. Offilius etiam ob eandem doctrinam Cesari fuit familiarissimus. Obscurior Labeo non euasit qui consulatum ab Augusto sibi mandatum proinde recusauit ut operam legibus liberius potiusque reparandis nauaret. Infiniti sunt alii qui uel ante, uel post natam christianitatem officiorum scriptione claruerunt. Quorum omnium non ideo meminimus quod de tuis laboribus aut singulari cum in omnes tum in me tua caritate uidear dubitasse, sed ut intelligas quo demum mea te uocat oratio qui cum moratissimis & clarissimis auctoribus illustre nomen meo nomine sis habiturus. Propones ergo teipsum tibi tot facultatibus ornatum. Propones uirtutis ornamenta quæ cum ceteris tum illustribus & officiosissimis Marchionibus tuis Badensibus inde nascentur infinita. Propones decus & nomen quod uni tibi, unus, breuis, expeditusque cursus suppeditat atque magis ac magis in horas accumulat. Vale.

Apud Turonem, edibus hospiti mei Radulfi Toustani ciuis longe humanissimi. Anno uno & septuagesimo quadringentesimoque supra Millesimum, Nonis Martii citissime scriptum.

Ioanni Lapidano Tetrastichon fichæteum.

Vt puncti, cesi pateant libri Ciceronis
Guillermi suasu, sis Lapidane uigil
Sic facili cursu, cum fruger, tum decus esse
Tu poteris semper, clara Fichetea spes.

X.

CICERO DE OFFICIIS.

Letter of Heynlin to Fichet.

Io. de Lapide sacris in litteris Parisii licentiatus, G. Ficheto parisiensi theologo doctori S. P. D.

Utrum potius tibi gratias agam eloquentissime ac doctissime pater, an mox aggrediar quod litteris tuis iubes, magna mihi sane dubitatio est. Nam (ut eloquentissimi scriptores tuique simillimi solent) tanti me uerbis tuis fecisti ut non referre solum uicissitudinem gratiamque nequeam (quemadmodum par in primis fuisset) sed etiam admodum reformido ne plus equo mihi tribuisse uidearis. Quo fit ut neque nunc tibi gratias agam qui nequeo, neque de me tot tantaque scribenti prorsus assentiar qui me meaque longe minora cognosco, neque quantum a te patre prestantissimo quotidie magis diligar & amer nesciam qui non qui sim, sed incredibilem erga me tuam caritatem ex uerbis tuis coram intueor. Non etiam supra quam tibi parere cuiquam debeo, quem mihi semper ad optima queque ducem auctoremque proposui. Et ne mihi quidem ab re sic fecisse uideor. Eas nanque laudes quibus ad emendanda & distinguenda Ciceronis officia me prosa uersibusque prosequeris, mutuatas a te profiteor qui theologiam nedum philosophiam annos complures, illam quidem in his sorbonensibus edibus & hanc in stramineo uico Parisii docuisti, qui prioris sorbonensis, rectoris parisiensis, nunc regii, nunc apostolici legati munus & officium cumulata laude gessisti, qui de studiis humanitatis ea scripsisti, sæpe sæpiusque docuisti quæ (ut de te grauissimus pater Nicenus cardinalis Bessario scribit) cum optent Athenienses, tum mirentur Romani. Mea uero sententia quam Apollonius Rhodius singularem de Cicerone laudem predicauit, nunc apud Gallos tuam sane fecisti. Nam ut eloquentiam e Grecis in Latium Cicero primus omnium cumulatissime traiecit, sic e Latio Luteciam, eam tu longe primus intulisti. Quam quidem ob rem (ut egregiis de te carminibus Gaguinus perscripsit) Te digne extulerit preclara Lutecia celo cui tua rectiloquos lingua diserta parit. Ita ne mirum quidem mihi uidetur (quom sis orator, quem uirum bonum dicendique peritum finit

Cato, quemque Ciceronis officia reddere possunt) si nunc eorum emendationem distinctionemque litteratorie mihi imponis quorum studio cæteros tui fore persimiles arbitraris et optas. At uero pater arduum sane debili recusareque non audenti munus imponis. Quod si fragiles humeros concusserit aut fortassis aliquando tandem in totum oppresserit, tua sit culpa qui quem ferre non possum meis humeris fascem apponis. Sin uel egerrime particulatimque (ut imbecilles plerique conantur) tantum onus quo iubes sustulero. Tua sane sit laus egregia qui quom tempestate penitus exulant officia meis humeris ad Gallos reportanda credideris. Non itaque quam docte sed quam libenter tuis obediui preceptis, equidem spectes qui non Ciceronis tantum officia, uni **tibi frugalitatis** & officiorum amantissimo patri pro uiribus emendaui, rubrisque capitulatim seiunxi, sed (ut amoris usuram tibi redderem) Lælium, Catonem Sextumque de Republica (quod somnium Scipionis dici solet) emendatos pariterque seiunctos tue tantum summitto trutine grauissimoque iudicio, atque ut breui ferre tota de re sententiam possis summam quandam mearum partitionum (quam uulgo tabulam dicunt) tanquam librorum omnium commentarium in operis uestibulo disposui quam mox istis oculis equissimis tuis iudicibus subiitio (sic). Vale.

Aedibus Sorbone Parisii scriptum.

Io. Lapidani Tetrastichon ad Guillermum Fichetum.

Accipe distinctos Guillerme libros Ciceronis.
Si lesi pateant, criminis auctor eris.
Sin fuerint frugi, maior tibi quam Lapidano
Gratia debetur, laus quoque maior erit.

XI.

RODERICUS, SPECULUM VITÆ HUMANÆ.

Letter of presentation to Robert d'Estouteville, Provost of Paris.

Epistola Recommendatoria.[1]

Magnifico militi domino Roberto de Estoteuille[2] preposito Parisiensi et **christianissimi** francorum regis Cambellario, impressores Parisienses seipsos perpetuo seruituros humiliter offerunt.

Si munus tua prestantia dignum offerre tibi possemus, clarissime miles, existimaremus profecto nos fore longe foelicissimos. Quippe qui nos ea benignitate prosequeris ut non agere sed ne uix quidem gratias habere tibi possimus. Et quidem quas ingentes tue debemus nobilitati. Non enim in hac ciuitate (quæ tuo regitur arbitratu tuisque

---

[1] Title not printed, but written in red.
[2] Robert d'Estouteville, fifth son of Guillaume d'Estouteville, Lord of Torci, was Lord of Beyne and St. André in the province of the Marche, Provost of Paris in 1446, counsellor and chamberlain to the kings Charles VII. and Louis XI. He assisted at the battle of Montlheri in 1465, and died on the 3rd of June, 1479.

seruatur, et augetur beneficiis) ut hospites et aduene, sed ut liberi et ciues a te tractamur, a tua magnificentia libertate donamur. Ita tibi gratias agant ceteri quas uolent quasque maximas poterunt. Nos equidem profitemur ingenue, uoluntatem tibi deditissimam nobis adesse, maioremque semper affuturam, referendi autem facultatem prope nullam. Atque ut huius nostre uoluntatis extet apud te nonnullum indicium, munusculi quiddam tuæ destinamus offerimusque prestantie, quod profecto speramus tibi maxime conducturum gratumque futurum. Est enim humane speculum uite his fere diebus a doctissimo patre Rodorico zamorensi episcopo Rome conditum editumque nuperrime. Quod potissimum tua causa, nunc omnibus Parisiis quam emendatissimum impressimus, ut qui te certo scimus de moribus uariisque statibus hominum (quos opus istud omnes particulatim districat) libenter lecturum. Ea nanque perlegimus auidius que cognitu dignissima usuque iudicamus oportuna. Atqui nullus est uel latissimi princeps imperii cui plures et dissimiliores quam tibi sint mores pernoscendi. Omnis nempe status, omnis professio, omnisque natio, tanquam in orbe quodam, in urbe Parisea præposito tibi proponitur, tuoque paterno subicitur imperio. Etenim nunc ea uidetur Parisiorum ciuitas quæ quondam Roma fuit, quam qui uidissent, non urbem quidem aliquam, sed ipsum terrarum orbem se plane fatebantur intuitos. Quin ut cyneas Pyrrhi legatus ipsi epyrotarum regi de urbe Roma interroganti respondit, ciues romanos omnes senatores, urbem senatum, ipsum denique senatum sibi regum conuentum uideri. Nos quoque nunc eadem de ciuitate (quam sapientissime iustissimeque gubernas) loqui possumus. De te uero tanquam de altero Fabricio, qui tum Romæ summus in Re Publica princeps erat, cum elogium illud singulare quidem de Romana Re Publica Pyrrho cyneas coram dixit. Suscipies itaque fructiferum tibi iocundum a tuis mancipiolis obseruantie nostre pignus. Tuorum quidem, cum in omnes, tum in nos ipsos iustitiæ et beneficentiæ meritorum **monumentum**. Vale.

> Que tua nos pietas conseruat clare Roberte
> Suscipiat munus quod tibi sit placitum.

XII.

RODERICUS, SPECULUM VITÆ HUMANÆ, 1472.

Letter of presentation to the Duke Jean de Bourbon.

Epistola Commendatoria.[1]

Inuictissimo principi Iohanni bourbonii [2] atque aluernie duci, comiti Claromontensi, forensi, insulæque Iordane, domino bellioci, pari atque camerario franciæ, librorum Parisii impressores germani sese perpetuo seruituros liberalissime offerunt.

Etsi scimus, illustrissime dux, nos indignos esse quibus tua ducalis dignitas ita se

---

[1] This title is not printed, but written in red by a contemporary hand.
[2] Jean II., Duke de Bourbon and Auvergne, Count of Clermont, Forez, and Isle-en-Jourdain, Lord of Beaujeu, peer and great chamberlain of France, surnamed by his contemporaries "Le Bon." Died on the 1st of April, 1488.

humanam facilemque præbeat, ut nos externos tibique ignotos tua humanitate (quæ summa est) prosequereris, non tamen satis mirari possumus tantam in tanto principe quantum omnis te gallia admiratur pietatem, ut humiles nostras casas, stridentesque impressorias formulas cum parisii esses sponte uisendo ad laborem reddere uolueris alacriores et eas ita iocundissimo tuo intuitu reficere ut sese foelices formas cuncta in secula futuras sperarent. Obseruas princeps foelicissime egregium illud philosophorum dictum, quanto superiores sumus, tanto nos geramus summissius. Nam cum inter christianissimi huius regni principes dignissimus sis, et summus ipse deus summa tibi corporis animique bona cumulatissime dederit, tamen ita te cunctis humanum, pium, placabilem, mitemque ostendis, ut solus is tue beniuolentie, beneficentiæ atque magnificentiæ copiam non habeat qui non digne petierit. Quare illud uere dici in te a nobis potest, dux inclyte, quod lysandrum lacædemonium Cyro minori persarum regi dixisse Cicero scribit, cum ad eum uisendum Sardis uenisset ; recte (inquit) Cyre, te beatum homines ferunt quoniam uirtuti tue fortuna coniuncta est. Tu uero longe felicior es cyro. Quippe cum te uultus honestat, non dedecorant mores, cum te animus iustitiam in homines et pietatem in deos colens ornat, non te destituit corpus. Bellis insignis es, nec uitiis pacem foedas. Resplendes gloria martis et plus egisti inermis. Sed quid nos parum docti laudum tuarum precones esse nitimur, o dux, o princeps, o galliæ commune decus? Prodeant domestici tui uiri doctissimi qui maiores ac pene diuinas in te sitas extollant uirtutes. Euocet e cælo suo sibique notissimis astris Conradus ille tuus astrorum, medicine, omniumque disciplinarum peritissimus camenas, que te dignas per secula laudes modulentur. Nos uero cum pro summa tua in nos humanitate pares tuo nomini gratias non referre sed ne quidem agere ualemus. Primum nos totos tue magnificentie iamdudum deditos, iterum atque iterum dedimus, ut nobis ex tua sententia ducalis tua dignitas semper utatur. Deinde si quid nostro labore, studio atque industria hoc in regno (te duce) foelicissimo ualemus, id omne ad celebrandum illustrandumque clarissimum tuum nomen omni studio conferemus. At uero ut integerrime nostre uoluntatis aliquod faciamus periculum, suscipies frugiferum tibique (ut speramus) non futurum iniocundum operis nostre munusculum : humane speculum uite, his pene diebus a doctissimo patre Rodorico zamorensi episcopo romæ conditum. Quod omnium reipublice rectorum nomine (quorum tu, et dux et princeps et moderator es) impressimus, quo uarios hominum multorum status atque mores dinoscerent, quos liber hic officiosissime perstringit.

XIII.

RODERICUS, SPECULUM VITÆ HUMANÆ.

Letter of presentation to the King.

Epistola commendatoria principi.[1]

Principibus posse placere, non ultimam uiris esse laudem philosophorum testatur sententia, rex inclyte. Qua inducti, nos longe futuros speraremus foelicissimos, si

[1] Title not printed, but written in red.

nostra industria muneris quippiam regali tua maiestate dignum et effingere et formatum regie tue sublimitati satis digne possemus offerre quo tibi primario huius regni principi placuisse nostris animis id expetentibus lætari ualeremus. Quippe qui tanta in nos beneficentia es ut nihil unquam satis dignum tuæ magnificentie aut agere aut referre possimus. Nam (ut diuinas regii tui sceptri laudes nobis doctioribus extollendas relinquamus) tanta est in te, tum in omnes, tum in nos pietas atque clementia, ut alii regia tua benignitate placidissime foueantur, nos uero in regni tui principe urbe parisia, non ut inquilini, non ut incole, non ut hospites sed ut concíues liberi tractemur, et ita quidem benigne ut nusquam nobis gratior extet libertas quam sub te rege piissimo, qui sola tua freti clementia libris imprimendis regnum hoc te rege fœlicissimum illustrare magnopere desyderamus. Quo studio etsi placere tibi non satis digne ualemus, profitebimur tamen ingenue, uoluntatem nobis summam non deesse regie tue sublimitati inseruiendi, maiorem semper affuturam, facultatem autem prope nullam. Quid enim summo principi gratum satis agant externi, humilesque artis impressorie professores ? Quid potentissimo regi, inopes ? Summa tamen innata tibi pietas audaciam nobis prestat nos, nostramque industriam regiæ celsitudini tuæ dedicandi, rex clementissime. Nempe quid te monet uel pœnis hominum uel sanguine pasci, turpe fœdumque putare ? Clementia tibi innata. Quid facit ut deponas ocius iram quam moueas ? Summa in te clementia, quæ te deo proximum efficit. Quid tandem te docet precibus nunquam inplacabilem esse, obuia prosternere, prostrataque leonis instar despicere ? Clementia. Hac das ueniam uictis, rex inuictissime. Hac exortante, martis horrificos coerces calores, etherei patris imitatus exemplum, qui sonoro tonitrui cuncta concutiens, cyclopum spicula in scopulos et monstra maris e summa cæli arce iaculatur, nostri parcus cruoris. At uero (dignissime rex, cuius laudem uox humana non capit) ut tibi non quas debemus, sed quas possumus gratias agamus, nostre quoque uoluntatis quam spondemus semperque exhibebimus emineat apud te aliquod indicium, obseruantiæ nostræ pignus, quod nostris effinximus manibus, tibi offerimus summa cum reuerentia. Sperantes id tue benignitati non ingratum futurum. Est nanque Vite speculum humanæ, in quo et regii tui solii et hominum tuo sceptro subiectorum uarios casus, uaria quoque rerum discrimina quandoque per ocium non summo sine fructu, maiore cum iocunditate speculabere. Quod suscipias oramus a nobis tuis mancipiolis, non pro numeris specie quod perquam exiguum est, sed pro animi nostri uoluntate quo **regium tuum** numen obseruare, uenerari et colere studemus, semperque maiorem in modum[1] studebimus. Tua in Lutetia, x kal. **maii** Anni millesimi quadringentesimi secundi supra septuagesimum, manibus tibi deditissimorum Martini, Vdalrici atque Michaelis impressum.

   Christianissimo francorum regi diuo Ludouico quarto (*sic*) Germani librorum impressores Parisienses perpetuo se deuouent seruituros.

[1] Printed " immodum."

XIV.

PLATONIS EPISTOLÆ.

Letter of presentation to Jean Choard.

Guillermus **Fichetus** Parisiensis **theologus doctor Iohanni Choardo cancellario** Calabrie uiro clarissimo salutem.

Magni diuinique Platonis epystolas meo nomine iussi tibi reddi quas ad reipublicæ rectionem magno tibi fore adiumento non dubito. Si tamen (quod te facturum certe cognosco) eas crebra lectio tibi familiares reddiderit, has si quidem ut tibi uel domi uel ruri facile in manibus essent enchyridionis instar transcribi feci. Ac ne fortassis ut soles de referenda gratia pluribus agas aut cauponari mecum amicitiam contendas, non equidem te sed in qua tu commode uersaris rempublicam platonicis meis epystolis dono. Rogo pace tua dicam quod ingenue do, mutua nostra necessitudine sentio. Si pergis mercatorio more mecum agere et res rebus ultra citraque librare, nunc profecto finem fecisti amicitie nostre. Vale. Iam explodor tua domo. Sin meo me more uersari tecum patieris, non alii solum egregii mei scriptores apud te platonem sequentur, sed etiam ego quom dabitur occasio te tuisque copiis longe maioribus utar. A quibus aperte sane me reiicis nisi gratis meus Plato tecum fuerit exceptus hospitio. Vale et fortunis te serua secundis. Apud parisiensem Sorbonam quinto Kalendas maias scriptum.

Disticon ficheteum.

Ite mee platonis opes ad uota Ioannis
Vultu qui placido uos quoque suscipiet.

(Bibliothèque Nationale, Latin MSS., N° 16,580.)

FACSIMILES.

GVILLERMVS Fichetus parisiensiũ theologus doctor, Ioanni Lapidano Sorbonensis scholæ priori salutem ;
Misisti nuper ad me suauissimas Gasparini pergamensis epistolas, nõ a te modo diligent emẽdatas: sed a tuis quoqʒ germanis impressoribus nitide & terse trã/ scriptas. Magnam tibi gratiã gasparinus habeat. quem pluribus tuis uigiliis ex corrupto integrʒ fecisti. Maiorẽ uero cæ/ tus doctorʒ hoĩmʒ qʒ nõ tm sacris litteris. (quæ tua prouicia est)magnopere studes? sed redintegrãdis etiã latinis sc̃ptoribus insignem operam nauas. Res sane te uiro doctissimo & optimo digna. ut q̃ cũ lau/ de & gloria sorbonico certamini dux p̃ fuisti: tum latinis quoqʒ lris quas(ætatis̃ nostræ ignoratio tenebris obumbrauit) tua lumen effundas industria. Nam præt alias complures Iræʒ grauiores iacturas, hanc etiã acceperũt: ut librarioʒ uitiis, effectæ pene barbaræ uideant. At uero

LETTER OF FICHET TO HEYNLIN.
(DOCUMENT I.)
FROM THE "EPISTOLÆ GASPARINI."

91

re intelligā amari? nullū ego modū offi/
ciīs meis, aut amori meo in illū faciā. Sed
ne ab ōnibus te deſertū eſſe iudices? ego
(quem forte in numero amicoᵣ nō habe/
bas) polliceor tibi opera meā. & (qđ illi
non ſine ſcelere neglexerūt) ego paratus
ſum defenſionē tuam ſuſcipere . Tu uero
admonebis, quibus adiumentis opus tibi
ſit. & ego neq̃ pecunia? neq̃ conſilio tibi
deero . Vale ?

  Foelix Epſtarᵣ Gaſparini finis,

Vt ſol lumen? ſic doctrinam fundiſ in orbem
 Muſarum nutrix, regia pariſiuſ ?
Hinc prope diuinam, tu quā germania nouit
 Artem ſcribendi? ſuſcipe promerita,
Primos ecce libroſ? quos hæc induſtria finxit
 Francorum in terriſ . ædibuſ atq̃ tuiſ ?
Michael Vdalricuſ, Martinuſq̃ magiſtri
 Hoſ impreſſerunt . ac facient alioſ;

LAST PAGE, WITH COLOPHON, FROM THE
"EPISTOLÆ GASPARINI."

GVILLERMVS fichetus Parisiensis theologus doctor, Roberto Gaguino, uiro doctissimo salutem;

Magna me uoluptas capit eruditissime Roberte, quū musas, & omēs eloqn̄tiæ partes (quas por ætas ignorauit) in hac urbe florere conspicio. Nam ut me primū adolescētibus annis, borco ex agro luteciam contuli (idq̓ Aristoteleæ disciplinæ causa) mirabat sane oratorē, aut poetā phœnice ratiorē lutecia tota inueniri. Nemo Ciceronē (uti plenq̓ nūc faciūt) nocte̅a uersabat manu-uersabat diurna. Nemo carmē fingebat legitimū. nemo fictū ab alio, cæsuris nouerat librare suis. desuefacta siqdem a latinitate schola parisiensis, ad sermonis rusticitatem, omīs pene deciderat. At lapillo longe meliore dies nostri numerant. quippe quibus di, deæq̓ omēs (ut poete loquūt) benedicēdi artes, indies magis magisq̓ aspirant. Siq̓ dem (ut missos faciam alios) tu usqueadeo musis, & omi carmīs genere p̄stas: ut si non solū illi qdē uates nobilissimi (tibulus, Lu

LETTER OF FICHET TO GAGUIN, P. 1.
(DOCUMENT II.)
FROM THE "ORTHOGRAPHIA."

crecius, Horatius, Naso, Statius, Lucanus, Marcialis, Persius, Iuuenalis) sed etiā lōge princeps Virgilius, ab helisceis campis ad nos remearent. pfecto tuū carmē suū esse ar bitrarent. Quid enī Maroni tuo carmīe si/ milius? quod de Ludouico rege nostro for// tissimo, pximis diebus cecinisti? Quid illo quadratius? quod dialogoɤ instar, unū aut alteɤ effinxisti? Taceo ciuitatis pariseæ lau des. quæ adeo sūt a te uerboɤ uenustate, & sentenciaɤ grauitate referte! ut utɤ utri laude p̄ferat. iudicare sit difficile. Pręterco quæ de galliæ hyspaniæcɋ prestantia soluta pr̄one scripsisti. Nō enī est huius tēporis, de tuis studiis, p̄sertim ad te scribere. De studi/ oɤ humanitatis restitutōe loquor. Quibus (q̄tū ipse coniectura capio) magnū lumē no uoɤ librarioɤ genus attulit. quos n̄ra me/ moria (sicut qdam equus troianus) quoquo/ uersȯ efiudit germania. Feřūt enī illic, haut procul a ciuitate Maguncia, Ioannē quendā fuisse, cui cognomē bonemōtano. q p̄mus oīm impressoriā artē excogitauerit. q̄ nō calamo

(ut prisci qdem illi)neqʒ penna(ut nos fin
gimus)sed æreis lris libri fingunt· & qdem
expedite,polite,& pulchre·Dignus sane hic
uir fuit! q̃ omẽs musæ,omẽs artes,omsqʒ eoɪ̯
linguæ,q libris delectant! diuinis laudibʒ
ornent· eoq magis dis,deabusqʒ anteponãt!
quo ppius ac plentius lris ipsis,ac studiosis
homibus,suffragiũ tulit· Si qdem deificant
liber & alma ceres·ille qppe dona lici inue
nit, poculaqʒ inuctis achelois miscuit uuis.
hæc chaoniam pingui glandem mutauit ari
sta·Atq(ut poeta utamur altero)prima ce
res unco glebam dimouit aratro· prima de
dit fruges, alimentamitia terris · At bone
mõtanus ille, lõge gratiora diuiniotaqʒ in
uenit·quippe q lras eiusmoĩ excilpsit! qbus
quidquid dici,aut cogitari potest! propediẽ
scribi,ac trãscribi, & posteritatis mãdari me
moriæ possit · Neqʒ presertim hoc loco nr̃os
silebo·qui superãt iam arte magistrɪ̯· quorɪ̯
Vdalricus Michael ac Martinus principes
esse dicunt· q iam,pridẽ Gasparini pgamen
sis epistolas impresserunt! quas ioannes lapi

Letter of Fichet to Gaguin, p. 3.

danus emendauit. qn illius auctoris ortho͞-
g͞rphiā (quā hic etiā accurate correxit) se acci͞-
g͞ut perficere. opus mea qdem sentencia egregiū. necq͞ auribus solū iuuētutis g͞tissimū. sed
doctioꝝ quocq͞ studiis oportunū. Nō eni͞ (qd
pace multoꝝ dictū esse uelim) ref est ortho-
g͞rphia fructu puo ac tenui. ueꝝ p͞grandi, gratissimo, appme necessario, & iocūdo. si qdē re͞-
cte scribēdi ratio (quā othog͞rphiæ sonat inī͞-
p͞tacio) nobis in oi ligua, grǝca latīa uernacla
q͞ suffragaē. qua sine nil emēdate, ac pure scri
bi, nil legi, nil nisi contorte esse͞m possit.
Quotū eni͞ quencq͞, siue grāmaticū, siue oratorē, siue philosophū excelluisse inuenias? qui
nō huic diuinæ arti maiorē inmodū studuerit? Nempe (ut hinc incipiā) didimus cū om͞e-
nē, tū hanc grāmaticǝ ptem libris q͞plurimis
exornauit. quo fit ut omibo artis grāmaticæ
,pfessoribo (quiqdem esset, ac fuisset) Macro-
bio eū iure p͞tulerit. Nigidius (quoq͞ cui figulo fuit cognome͞) anli Gelii sentēcia scdm
Marcū Varrone͞ locū est consecuto. Cur ita?
nimiꝝ q͞ multus in orthog͞rphiæ præceptio͞e

LETTER OF FICHET TO GAGUIN, P. 4.
(For conclusion see pp. 73-75.)

Caii Crispi Salustii de Lucii
Catilinæ coniuratione liber
fœliciter incipit.

OMNIS homines qui sese studẽt
præstare cæteris animalibus sũma
ope niti decet. ne uitam silentio
transigant, ueluti pecora. quę natura prona atq̃
uentri obedientia finxit. Sed nostra omnis uis
in animo & corpore sita est. animi imperio
corporis seruitio magis utimur. alterum nobis
cum dis, alteru cum beluis commune est. Quo
mihi rectius uidet̃. ingenii, q̃ uirium opibus
gloriã q̃rere. &(quoniã uita ipa qua fruimur
breuis ẽ) memoriã nri q̃ maxime longã efficere
Nam diuitiaru & formę gla fluxa atq̃ fragilis
est. uirtus clara æternaq̃ habetur. Sed diu
magnũ inter mortales certamẽ fuit. ui ne cor
poris. an uirtute animi, res militaris magis p
cederet. Nã priusq̃ incipias. ꝯsulto. & ubi ꝯsu
lueris. mature facto opus est. Ita utrũq̃ p se
indigens. alteru alterius auxilio eget. Igit̃
initio reges(nam in terris nomen imperii id

FIRST PAGE OF THE "SALLUST."

est·quo metu omīs **italia** contremuerat·Illicq̃
& inde uſcq̃ ad noſtrã memoriã romani ſic ha/
buere·Alia omīa uirtuti ſuæ ꝑna eſſe· Cum
gallis ꝑ ſalute.͡ nō ꝑ gloria certare ;

Ed poſtq̃ in numidia bellū confectū.͡ & Iu
gurthã uinctū adduci romã nūciatū eſt.͡ mari͜
us conſul abſens factus eſt·& ei decreta ꝓuī/
cia gallia·iſcq̃ kał·Iañ·magna gloria cōſul tri
umphauit·Ex ea tempeſtate ſpes atcq̃ opes ci/
uitatis in illo ſitæ ſunt ;

·C·C riſpi S aluſtii de bello Iugur-
thino liber fœliciter finit ;
De morte Iugurthę diſticon ;
Qui cupis ignotum, Iugurthæ noſcere letum.͡
Tarpeiæ rupis, truſus ad ima ruit ;

Nunc parat arma uiroſcq̃ ſit rex maximus orbis.͡
Hoſtibus antiquis exitium minitans·
Nunc igitur bello ſtudeas gens pariſeorum.͡
Cui martis quondam gloria magna fuit·
Exemplo tibi ſint nunc fortia facta uirorum.͡
Quæ digne memorat Criſpus in hoc opere·
Armigeriſcq̃ tuis alemannos adnumeres.͡qui
Hos preſſere libros arma futura tibi ;

LAST PAGE, WITH COLOPHON, FROM THE "SALLUST."

Epla Comedatoria

¶ Inuictissimo p̄ncipi Iohanni bourbonii atq̄ aluernię duci comiti claromontesi, forensi insulaeq̄ Iordanę, dn̄o belliio ci, pari atq̄ camerario franciae. libroꝝ Parisii impressores germani, sese ppetuo seruituros liberalissime offerunt.

¶ Etsi sumus illustrissime dux nos indignos esse, q̄bus tua ducal. dignitas ita se humanā facilemq̄ praebeat, ut nos externos, tibiq̄ ignotos tua humanitate (quae sūma est) psequereris: nō tn̄ satis mirari possumus, tantā in tanto principe, quantū ōnis te gallia admirat̄, pietatē, ut humiles nostras casas, stridētesq̄ impressorias formulas, cum parisii esses sponte uisendo, ad laborē reddere uolueris alacriores; & eas ita iocūdissimo tuo intuitu reficere, ut sese foelices formas cuncta in sęcula futura sperarent. Obseruas p̄ncep̄s foelicissime egregiū illud philosophoꝝ dictum, quanto supiores sumus, tanto nos geramus summissius. Nam cum inter chr̄istianissimi huius regni p̄ncipes dignissimus sis, & sumus ipse deus sūma tibi corporis aīmiq̄ bona cumulatissime dederit, tamē ita te cunctis humanū, piū, placabilē, mitemq̄ ostendis, ut solus is tuę beniuolentię, b̄nficentiae atq̄ magnificentiae copiam nō habeat, qui nō digne petierit. ¶ Quare illud uere dici in te a nobis potest dux inclyte, quod lysandū lacedaemoniū, Cyro minori persaꝝ regi dixisse Cicero scribit. cum ad eum uisendum Sardis uenisset, recte (inquit) Cyre te beatū hoīes ferunt, quoniā uirtuti tuę fortuna oiuncta est. Tu uero longe foelicior es cyro. Quippe cum te uultus honestat, nō dedecorāt mores, cum te animus iustitia in homines & pietatē in deos colens ornat, nō te destituit corpus. bellis insignis es, nec uitiis pacem foedas. Resplendes gloria martis, & plus egisti inermis; ¶ Sed quid nos paꝝ docti laudum tuaꝝ precones esse nitimur, o dux, o princeps, o galliae ōmune decus

DEDICATORY LETTER TO THE DUC DE BOURBON.
(DOCUMENT XII.)
FROM THE "RODERICUS ZAMORENSIS."

ALPHABET OF THE SORBONNE TYPES.

CORRIGENDA ET ADDENDA.

P. 6, l. 23, *for* 221 leaves, *read* 220 leaves.
P. 6, l. 27, *for* 237 leaves, *read* 236 leaves.
P. 17, l. 2, *for* 262 leaves, *read* 284 leaves.
P. 18, l. 13, *for* 124 leaves, *read* 126 leaves.
P. 18, l. 32, *for* first letter, *read* second letter.
P. 19, l. 8, *for* second letter, *read* first letter.
P. 50. *Add* to copies known of *Gasparini Epistolæ* : Bibliothèque de Rodez, imperfect.
P. 65. *Add* to copies known of *Juvenalis et Persius* a copy of the *Persius* only in the Grenville Library, British Museum, without the tetrastich at end.
P. 87, l. 7, *for* do, *read* de.

www.ingramcontent.com/pod-product-compliance
Lightning Source LLC
Chambersburg PA
CBHW020152170426
43199CB00010B/1004